The Hills of Circleville

Amy J. Cooper

Bloomington, IN 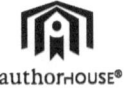 Milton Keynes, UK

authorHOUSE®

AuthorHouse™
1663 Liberty Drive, Suite 200
Bloomington, IN 47403
www.authorhouse.com
Phone: 1-800-839-8640

AuthorHouse™ UK Ltd.
500 Avebury Boulevard
Central Milton Keynes, MK9 2BE
www.authorhouse.co.uk
Phone: 08001974150

First published by AuthorHouse 2/16/2007

ISBN: 978-1-4259-8660-5 (sc)

Library of Congress Control Number: 2006911116

Printed in the United States of America
Bloomington, Indiana

This book is printed on acid-free paper.

This book is dedicated to Gregory P. Cooper.
Words elude me when I try to tell you how much I love you,
enjoy your companionship,
and how Blessed I feel that you have joined me in life's journey.

…to our dearest Lou Dewein.
How can Gregory and I ever thank you for showing us a better way to love life
and to appreciate Mother Earth. Thank you for the dream of Niches
and the courage to find our own small piece of heaven.

…für meinen Schwester, Wendy Walter.
You were my inspiration for the poetry for the Bradley Cancer Center. You
are my hero.

…to our special friend, Kay Breece.
Thank you for so enthusiastically helping us to explore Circleville.

…to Tom and Dorothy Cooper and Charlie and Linda Jackson.
Greg and I are touched by your friendship and grateful for how you have
shown us the beauty of the Pickaway, Hocking and Ross County areas
through history, art and music.

…to Keith and Terri Dumm.
Thank you for believing in me.
What great joy it brings me to have my books in your store, Something Different.

And thank you, Leah Pettit,
for ever so sweetly you always ask…"how is it coming?"

Special thanks to artists Mary T. Allen, Elizabeth Campbell and Gayle
Cummins for allowing me to use images of your art in this book. It is with
pleasure that I visit your work in the
Bradley Cancer Center at Berger Hospital and an honor to have my poetry
beside your art.

Wendy Elliott, thank you for inviting me to write poetry for the Bradley
Cancer Center, and thank you and Connie Kelly for extending the invitation
for me to write for Dr. Jain's practice in Grove City.

Michelle Callahan and the Pickaway County District Public Library,
thank you for sharing my love of books and joining me on my adventures.

Introduction

Throughout our lives, most of us are reaching for something intangible. In my life, it has been a search for a sense of home. "Are you going home for the holidays?" How do I answer that when I don't know where home is? I was born in Mansfield, Ohio. I love Ohio, and that love grew as I roamed the hills of this northern area. Skiing is a must in the winter, lakes are nearby for summer boating, and canoeing is a dream in the beautiful tree-lined rivers. This could have been home to me; but perhaps when I was younger, I needed more. I needed a better sense of family. And so my life traveled on.

While still young, my parents divorced and my sister, mother and I moved to Columbus, Ohio. I lived there for quite a few years. Much of the area is beautiful with trees and rivers. It is truly an interesting mix of nature's beauty and big city comforts. Restaurants, museums, theaters, and interesting areas like German Village, the Short North and more abound. The skyscape at night is breathtaking. I loved it...but I still wasn't home.

As a young adult, my life remained guided more by survival than by enjoyment. Through the years, I had continued a relationship with a woman who had been my mother's best friend. She always made me laugh and kept me filled with hope. I had had a crush on her son, Greg, since I was 5 years old. I lost touch with him through the years, and yet, through his wonderful mother, Dee, I always felt connected to him. One day, she decided to intervene. Unbeknownst to me, she included Greg in the plans we had made for dinner. Shortly thereafter, we began dating in that comfortable way that friends can do. Friendship, passion and love soon consumed us and we were married in December of 1992. Together, then, we began the search for a place where we would both feel at home. We knew we needed to live in the country, but also wanted to belong to a city where things felt intimate and we could be involved in the community. And so we began taking weekend journeys on one of Gregory's motorcycles …looking for home.

One day, it found us. Circleville, Ohio. The beauty of Circleville is in the people, in the historical downtown, in the surrounding land that is both flat and hilly, the rivers, streams, lakes, woods and farms. We fell in love with Pickaway County, Ohio and were fortunate to find jobs so we could work in the community where we live.

But alas, I have strayed…as you should know I often do. What I most want to share in The Hills of Circleville is how I have found and am in love with "home." From the moment we landed here at around midnight on November 2, 2003, my heart has been overwhelmed. I found "Home." I can answer that question now which had always eluded me, "I am already home for the holidays."

Circleville is in the perfect spot near beautiful parks for hiking and beautiful scenery. Pickaway County in and of itself is enough, so the bonus is that we are near the beautiful Hocking Hills, the hills of Ross County and Fairfield County. I hope that through these pages I have been able to portray a glimpse of the beauty and peace that consumes me. And I hope and wish for everyone a taste of this…this splendor of living in a place you love where even the most benign sights can inspire a lyric from the heart.

Contents

The Hills

...Of Circleville

The Love of God's Creatures

Poetry for the Bradley Cancer Center

Mashed Potatoes

Getting Here....

Living in Columbus, Ohio

It was unreal how quiet it could be in the mornings. The songs of the birds would cut a clear path through the sunbeams gently drying the dew from the grass. The sound of a distant dog barking would stir my heart. The peacefulness was matched only by the beauty of the large maples and pines which guarded my home from the weather, and from the busyness of the city. As calm as it was, it would quickly change as the day would awake. For this was life in the big city.

I never chose to live there. Growing up in a smaller city, Mansfield, in northern Ohio, I moved to the busy capital city of Columbus because I was only eight years old and divorce and a new man in my mother's life dictated where I would live.

This is not to say that I regretted it. It just wasn't my choice. Living in the 15th largest city in the United States certainly has its advantages. What a colorful array of friends to choose from. It gave me relationships that I will cherish for as long as I live. And the multicultural delicacies of dining in a melting pot society are beyond compare. Then there are the schools. How proud I am to say that I once lived in the city that is home to Ohio State University. How overwhelming it is to walk its campus and know that minds are being fed and the seeds of great ideas planted. It is here that research is being conducted that can change the world, if even to find a cure that saves only one life. I am always overwhelmed when at OSU that these things are occurring while I am in that space, on that campus.

While impressed with OSU, I knew that a smaller campus would be more suitable for me. How thrilled I was to be accepted into Capital University, at the age of 32, so I could begin my life long dream, my quest for a Bachelor's Degree. Working full time meant school had to wait for the evenings and the weekends. But how lovely those were, especially the evenings. The campus was so peaceful at night with a gentle breeze blowing as I safely walked to my car accompanied by the trees in their evening dance to the songs of the crickets.

After seven years, my degree in hand, I marched to the campus of Franklin University. Here I found another small campus and another rich education as I earned my Master's Degree. What a wonderful city that offered me all of this right in my own backyard.

My backyard, yes, that was truly my slice of heaven. I clung to those old trees for solace so many times after the death of Emily, my beloved dog. The breaking of my heart from her passing is something from which I shall never recover. Beyond my backyard, I found museums, bookstores, restaurants, and parks. Columbus is truly a place where you can find it all. And yet, my heart never felt at home; never felt it had a home. I yearned for something I did not know.

I found my peace when we moved to Circleville. Our little place in the country where the horse and donkey roam. Yes, I am grateful for all that the big city of Columbus gave me, but especially so for how it led me here. For my degrees helped me to find a better job and it was the search for that job that lead me to Circleville, Ohio.

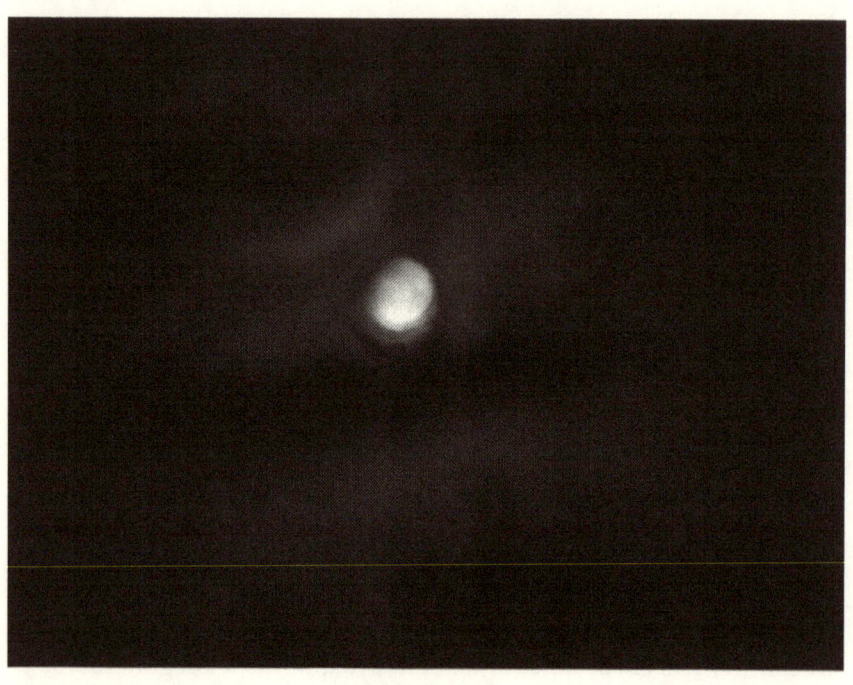

To Where
Scene from author's backyard - taken by Amy J. Cooper.

To Where

I know not where I'm coming from,
      Nor where I'm going to,
But I know if you take my hand, my love,
      That I will follow you.

To where'er the stars shall lead us,
      To where'er the moon does shine,
No boundaries to confine us,
      To where'er my love, divine.

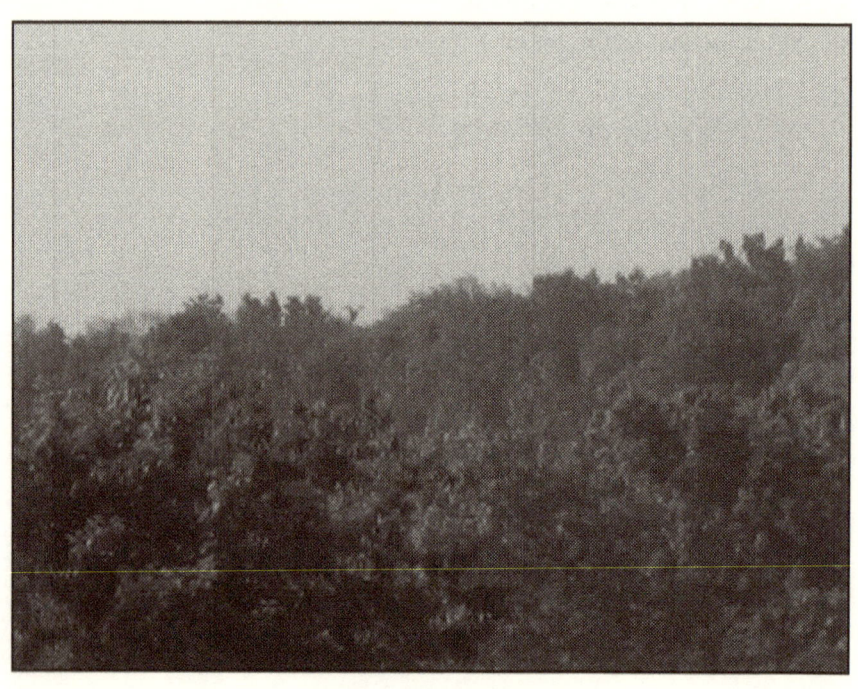

Where are you from?
Scene from author's backyard - taken by Amy J. Cooper.

Where are you from?

Here.

You were born here, then?

Not really.

But you say you are from here, right?

Yes.

So you've lived here all of your life?

Well, not in the physical sense.

I don't understand.

There isn't anything to understand.

It is as it has always been.

My heart, my mind and my soul have always been here.

Here....in the hills

    ....the Hills of Circleville.

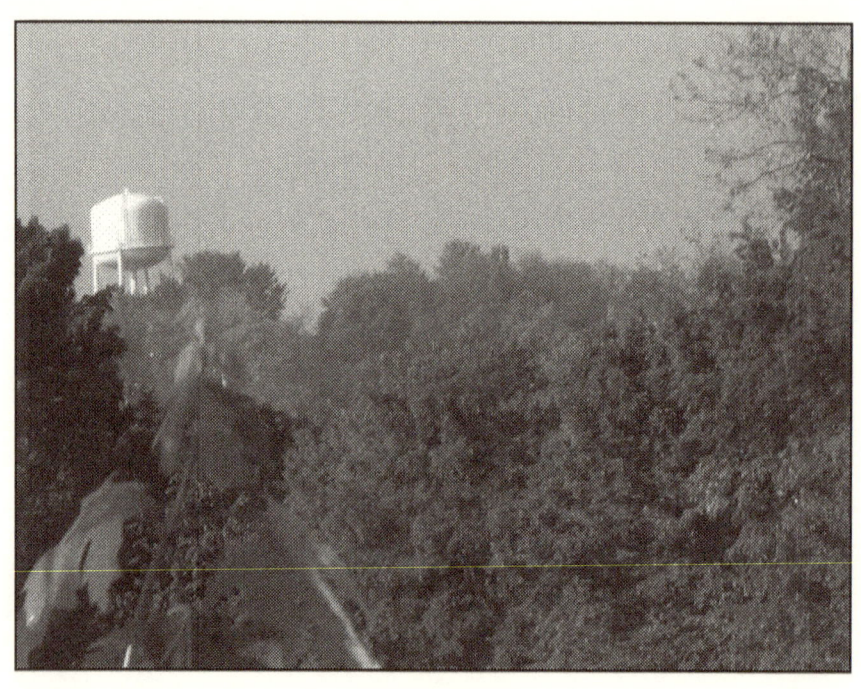

The Flatlander
Scene from author's backyard - taken by Amy J. Cooper.

The Flatlander

How could I think it?
  How would I have known?
    That long before I came here,
      The seed had been sown.

A flatlander's life,
  Full of hustle and strife,
    Was all that I knew,
      'til I dreamed of you.

My heart stirred with remembrance,
  As though I once knew,
    Rolling hills and fields,
      'neath the sky so blue.

Wherefrom came the memory,
  I do not know.
    But deep in my being,
      I knew it was so.

That the hills were calling,
  They were calling me home,
    To the hills of Circleville,
      To a place I'd not known.

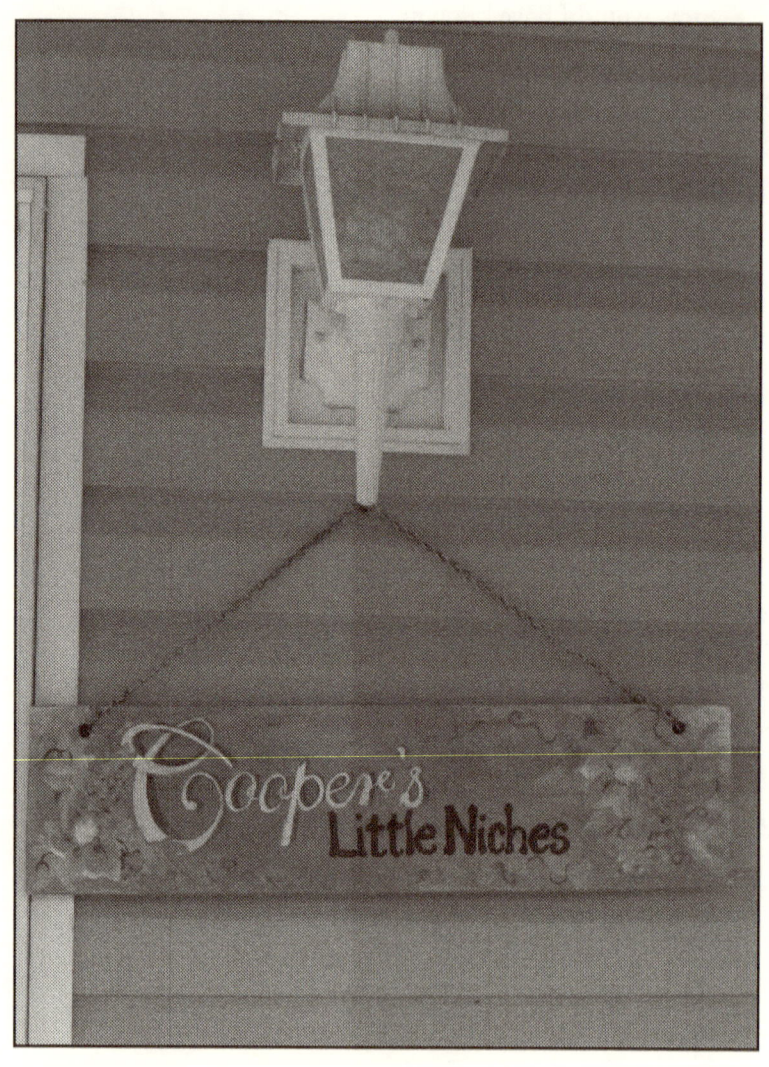

Photo: Finding Home
Scene from author's front porch - taken by Amy J. Cooper.

Finding Home

When Gregory and I were looking for our new home, we wanted to recreate our corner of the world as we had lived it vicariously through our friend, Lou, a scientist, a teacher, a friend of the earth – a Renaissance man. He created a piece of heaven in southeastern Ohio where people could retreat. That is putting it very simply. The truth is that Lou not only healed and protected land and wildlife, he set our souls on fire. So many lives have been changed simply because they have been touched by Lou.

Through Lou, we learned how important it is to have a place were you can go to find yourself. Sounds trite, I know, but when you can have a place to escape to that is tranquil and nurturing, the impact it can have on your being is truly astounding. Through Lou, we learned how important it is to be environmentally conscious. We wanted to find a place where we could help nature restore itself and where we could create a haven for plants and wildlife. We wanted a mini version of what Lou had, for we knew that we could never be as good at it as Lou, but we knew, as he had taught us, that every little thing we do to make a difference does.

We first saw home in the very beginning of our search. A sense of surrealism consumed me as I floated through the house and out into the expansive back with wood, stream and open land. Too soon to end a search we had just begun, we moved on. A couple of weeks later, Gregory and I decided to see if this house was still available. We called our representative from the realtors office, Lynn. She had become a friend through this journey and was excited that we felt we had perhaps found home. We made arrangements to return "home" one evening. It was the beginning of October and I remember standing at the front of the house listening to the night sounds and softly talking to Gregory about putting in an offer. That's when the geese came.

Several years ago, I had lost my companion, Emily Ann. To others she was a Dalmatian; to me she was the holder of my heart and the keeper of my dreams. She just happened to have spots. She saved my life once, but that is another story. Whenever the geese would fly overhead, Emily knew that I would take her to a park nearby where the birds liked to frolic in the pond. And so did we. Memories were made which always ended with us coming home covered in mud. To this day, whenever I hear the honk of the geese and see them flying over, I feel Emily nearby.

They came that night. The geese. And we knew. And we offered. And one month later, we moved into what we fondly call Cooper's Little Niches. Lynn had a sign made for us and gave it to us at the closing. I will forever be grateful to her for her kind patience in helping us find home. And I will always be grateful to Lou for helping us recognize home when we found it.

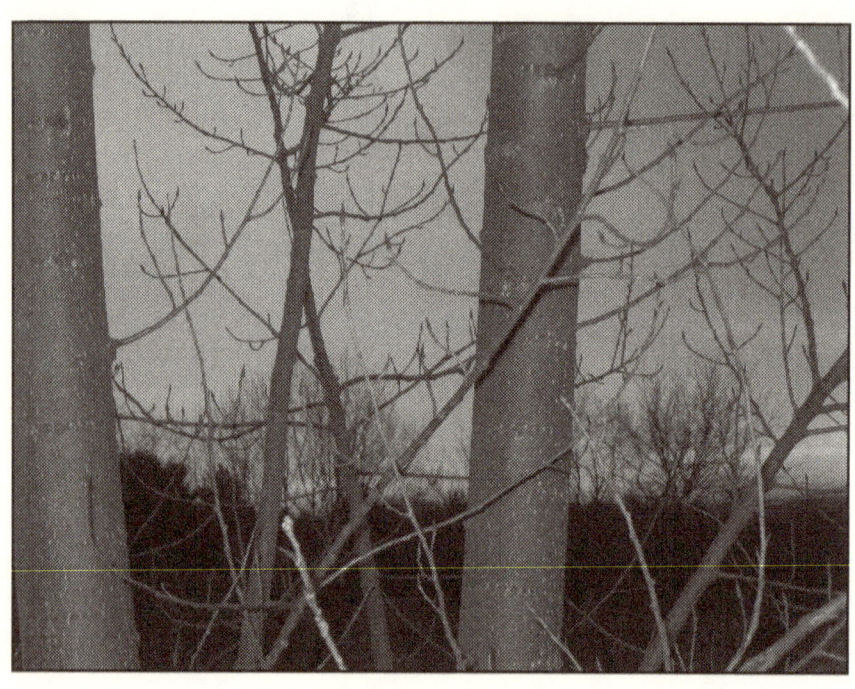

The Love of Emily
Scene from author's backyard - taken by Amy J. Cooper.

The Love of Emily

When early in the spring,
  And air is soft and cool,
    With a brush of winter's touch,
'Tis when I think of you,
  and how I miss you much.

For when the geese are on the wing,
  And rain makes mud of barren ground,
My head is filled with memories,
  And I feel your presence all around.

For oft we would run amongst the trees,
  And wade through rippling stream.
Two souls as one for all to see,
  In wake of day and night of dream.

Not only with the breath of spring,
  But on every day it seems,
I think the fluttering of wings I hear,
  And I feel your presence oh, so near.

For thoughts of you bring a tear,
  Not only in spring, but throughout the year.
A love never-ending, a love so strong,
  Forever I am blessed with the love of a dog.

Cooper's Little Niches

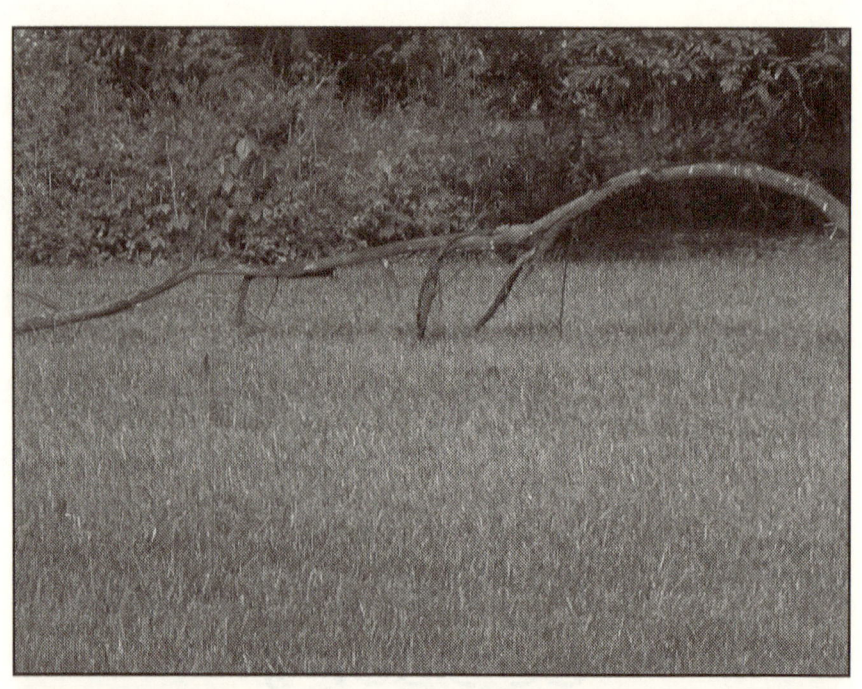

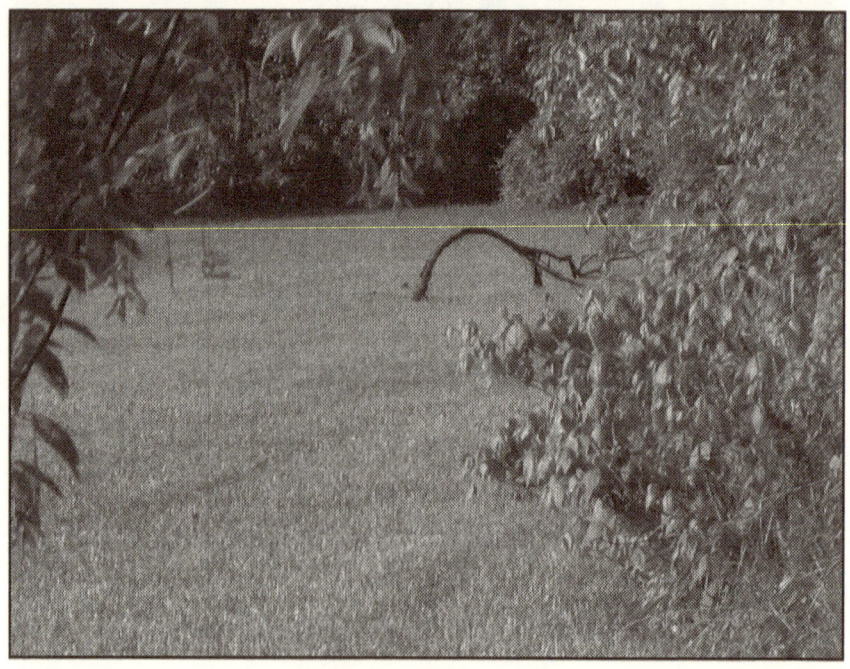

Nessy 1 and Nessy 2
Scenes from author's backyard - taken by Amy J. Cooper.

Nessy

Loch Nessy lives in my yard,
       I saw her there today.
She slowly moved around about,
       When I looked the other way.

I read of her years before,
       And so was quite surprised,
I thought she lived off another shore,
       Yet she was here before my eyes.

First she stood with head bent down,
       And nibbled on a seedling pine.
Then when she saw no one around,
       She moved on down the line.

Yes, Nessy lives in my yard.
       I saw her there today.
Perhaps one day you will see her,
       If you look the other way.

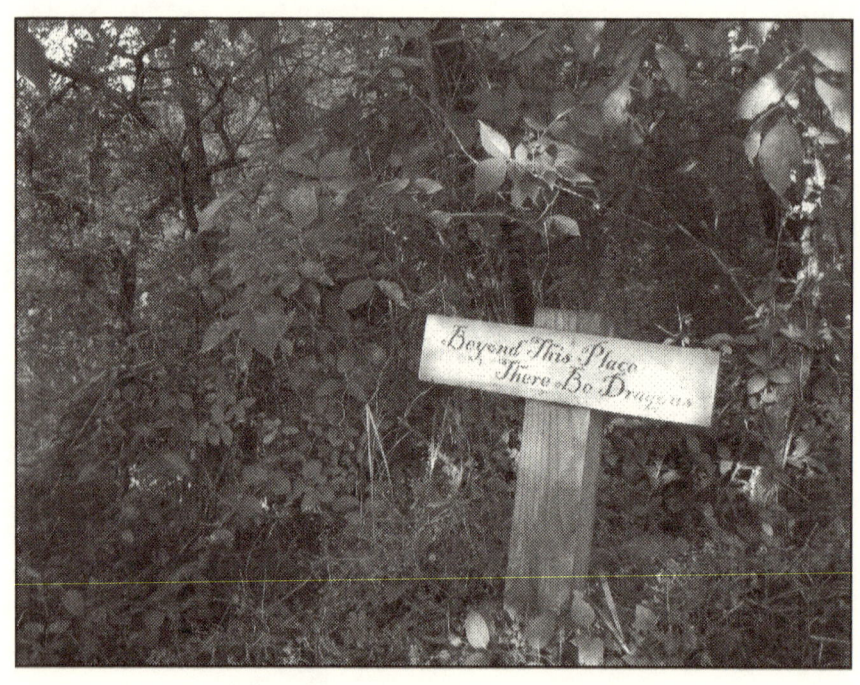

Beyond This Place There Be Dragons
Scene from author's backyard - taken by Amy J. Cooper.

Beyond This Place
There Be Dragons

Beyond this place, there be dragons.
      I believe it, for it's true.
For I've spent some time amongst them,
      And battled one or two.

Far more had approached me.
      Sometimes blind, I couldn't see,
That some who appeared friendly,
      Were truly mine enemy.

Yes, beyond this place the dragons be,
      This I know, I've felt their wrath.
But victory at last was mine you see,
      And ne'er again will they cross my path.

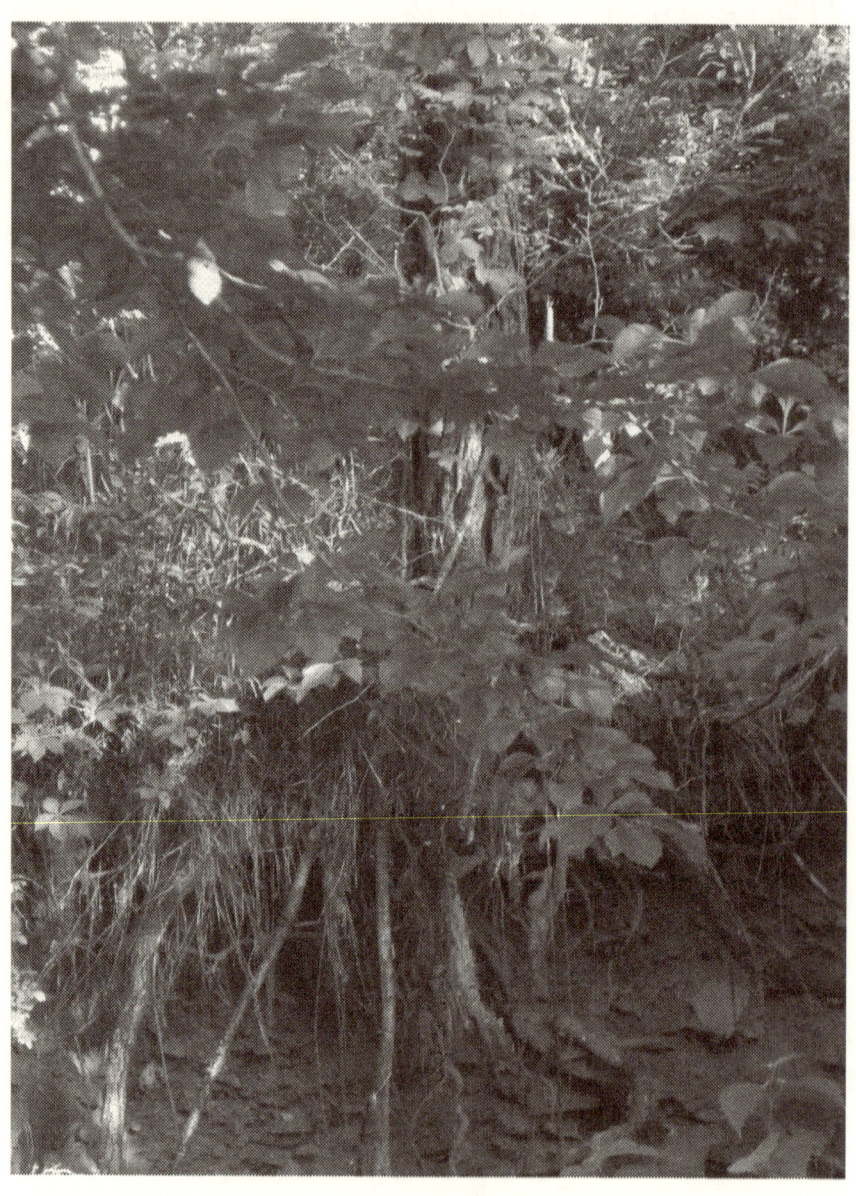

Family Ties
Scene from author's backyard - taken by Amy J. Cooper.

Family Ties

Though the miles and memories divide us,
      We cling to one another.
For the family blood that connects us,
      No stranger can tear asunder.

Our feet are rooted in the past,
      Though some memories wished not to last.
Our arms outstretched and open wide.
      We dream of reaching the other side.

For on that other side may be,
      Another pleasant memory,
Yet root bound we cannot leave,
      Paralyzed we stay and grieve.

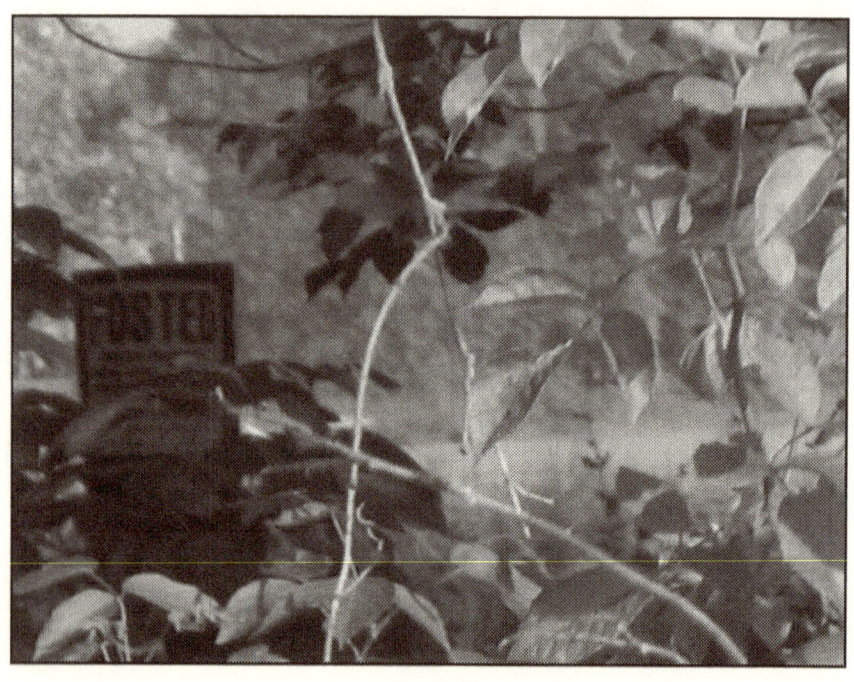

Posted
Scene from author's backyard - taken by Amy J. Cooper.

Posted

It's posted there.
    I saw the sign.
        To warn the wanderer,
            To not cross the line.

I'm standing here,
    The sign I've read,
        Beyond is fear,
            A fate to dread.

With respect I stand,
    And will not go,
        I'll not touch your land,
            With even a toe.

But signs like these are the tangible kind,
    Of warnings told and rules to follow.
        They cannot touch the intangible mind,
            Which chooses where to fly,
                And what to swallow.

...just a

I love this section because it touches on the hidden stories of the ordinary sights of our daily lives. We see a car abandoned in a stream, but it is so much more. It was the tool that helped one to see the country or it brought two lovers together. It is more than just an abandoned car. This is what The Hills of Circleville is to me. It is just a book, a collection of thoughts and impressions...just enough to fill these pages, but not enough to give you it all. I could write reams about this area and all that we have experienced since we have moved here. Instead, this is just my collection of some thoughts and some impressions. I could never capture it all. I am just a writer...

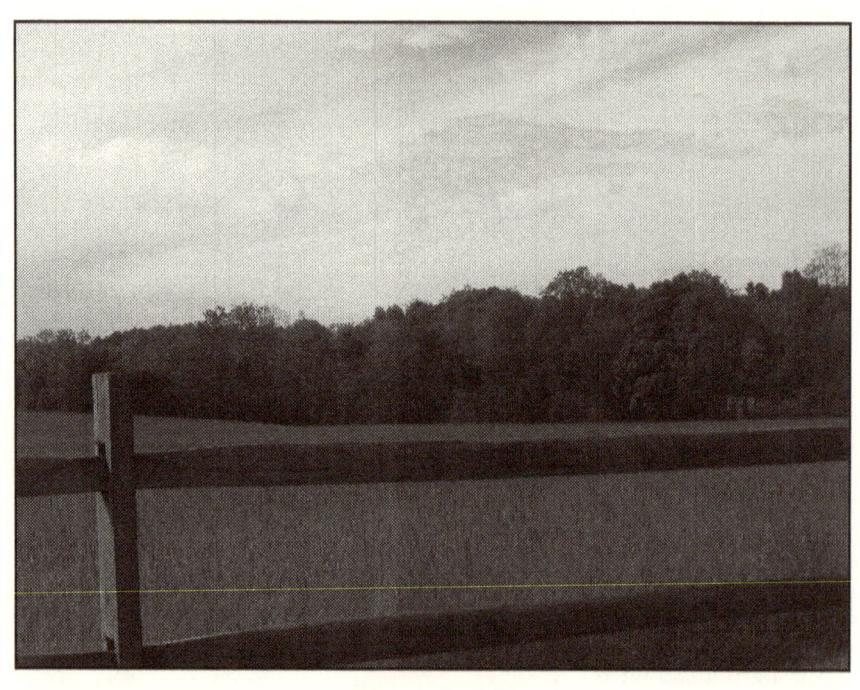

Just a Field
Scene from Moccasin Road - taken by Amy J. Cooper.

...just a

I am not faithful to you

    For I love another

        The lovely trees that caress her curves

            beckon me

        And so off I go

            Into the warm damp smell of her existence

...and when I am there

        I think of you

            And I tell her

I am not faithful to you

    For I love another

        The lovely trees that caress her curves

            beckon me

        And so off I go...

...Field

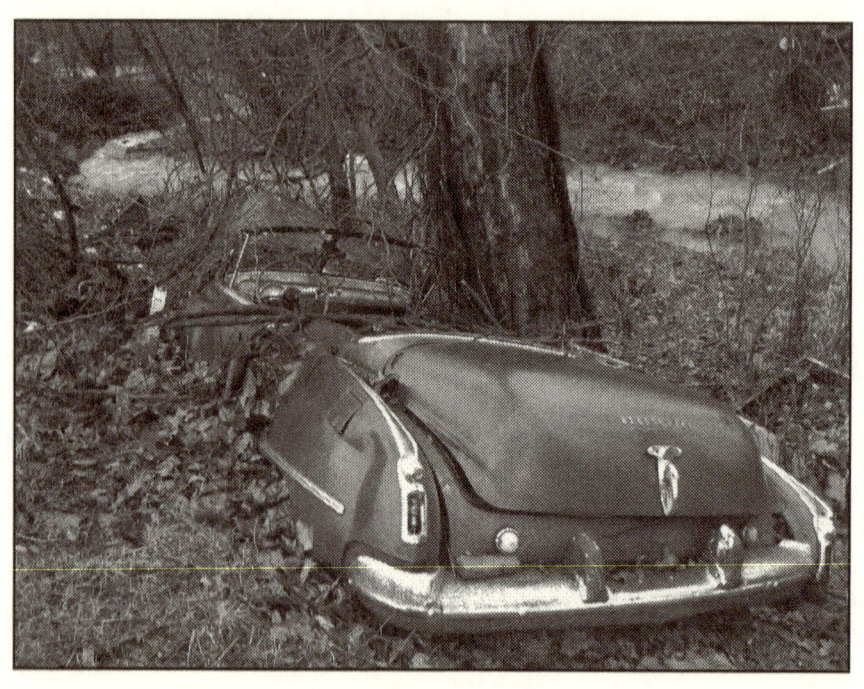

Just a 1949 Oldsmobile
Scene from author's backyard - taken by Amy J. Cooper.

...just a

I took him places
    He'd never been

I showed him sights
    He'd never seen

When he was afraid
    I held him safe

When he needed to run
    I gave him wind

And in the lonely of night
    I took him to her

When she gave birth
    I carried them home

For years I served
    For many have passed

And now I serve still
    Here by the stream
        Here by the tree
            Holding earth still
            I am

...1949 Oldsmobile

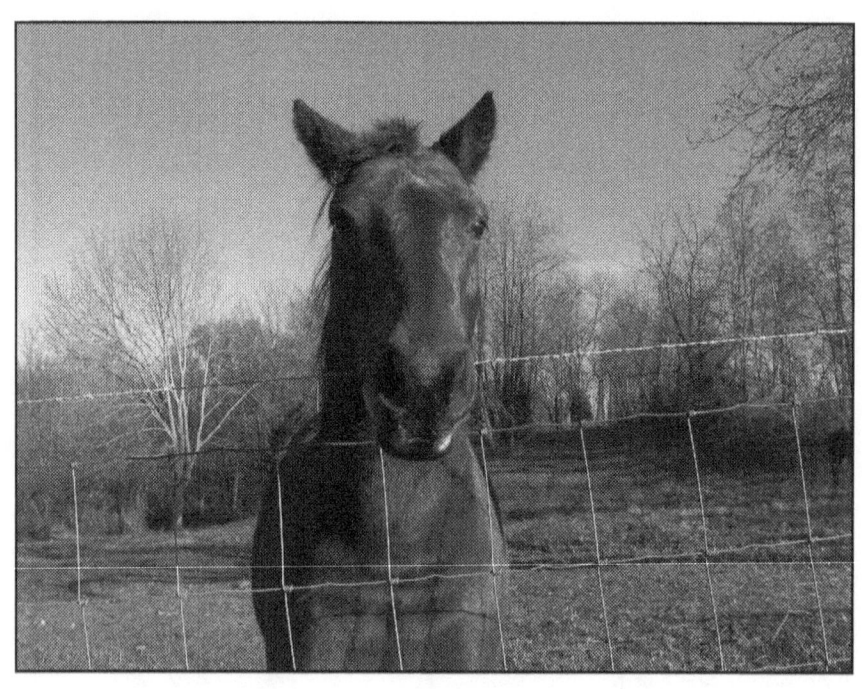

Just a Horse
View from author's front yard - taken by Amy J. Cooper.

...just a

Slowly I am flying
    With both feet on the ground
        One step at a time
            As a breath fights to breathe

I round the curve
    I see up ahead
        She's standing at the fence
            Her head held proud yet shy

I slow my steps
    I catch my breath
        Ah there's my beauty
            She stomps a hoof

Her eyes say she understands
    She lightly tosses her mane
        She turns
            And softly she flies
                With feet on the ground
                One step at a time
                    My breath fights to breathe

... horse

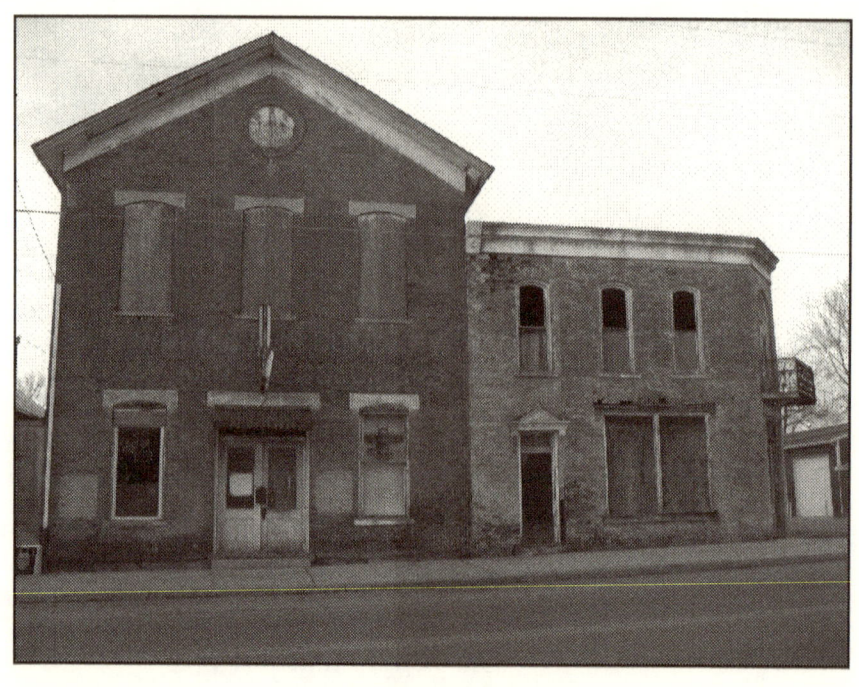

Just an Old Building
Scene from Tarlton, Ohio - taken by Amy J. Cooper.

Just an...

What memories do you hold,
　　　Of years gone by, of days of old?
What stories would you have to tell,
　　　If I should sit with you a spell?

I wonder how you came to be.
　　　Were you the dream of one, or of many?

How many stories would you unfold?
　　　How many more would remain untold,
Of days of honor and of glory?
　　　Tell me now, I crave your story.

Quiet and still I stand and wait,
　　　Afraid for a single breath to take,
So sure I am you'll begin to talk,
　　　I'm afraid to continue on my walk.

But alas your silence fills my soul,
　　　With mystery of tales untold.
So I'll move on and go my way,
　　　Sure to pause here another day.

...old building

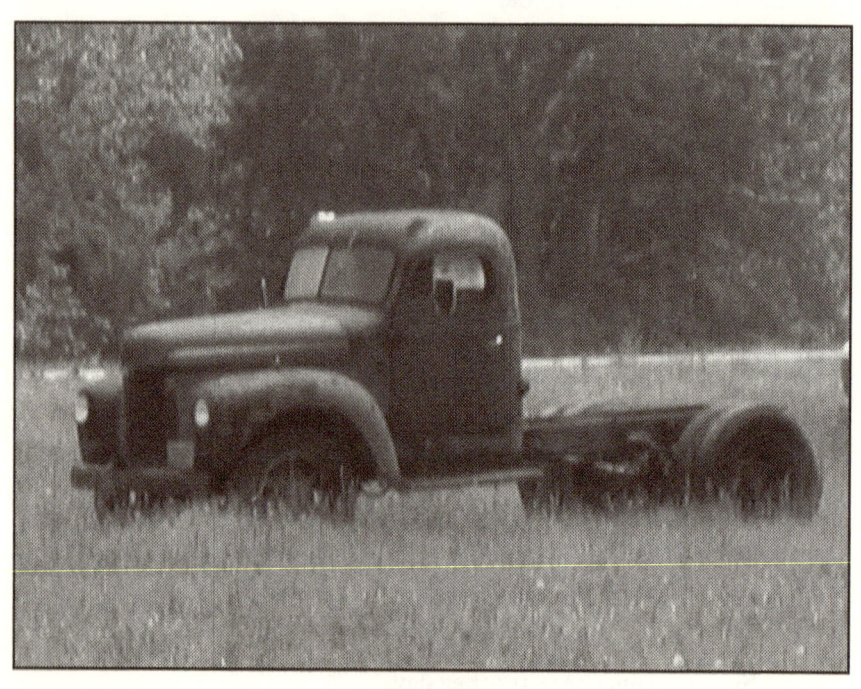

Just a Truck
Scene from Route 23, Pickaway County, Ohio - taken by Amy J. Cooper.

Just a....

I see you sitting there,
       Looking to the distance,
As though you've not a care.

But my heart can see right through,
       To the deep essence of you,
I know the being of your soul,
       I feel its mournful blue.

For once you drove the highway.
       For once you drove these roads.
And now you're on the byway,
       Ne'er again to carry loads.

I hear you speak, my heart is drunk,
       With memories of farmer's field,
For you are more than rusted junk.
       You worked the land, you carried yield.

I love the vision of you,
       And cherish your old tale.
The rust of honor is your badge.
       Much more than a truck left here for sale.

...truck

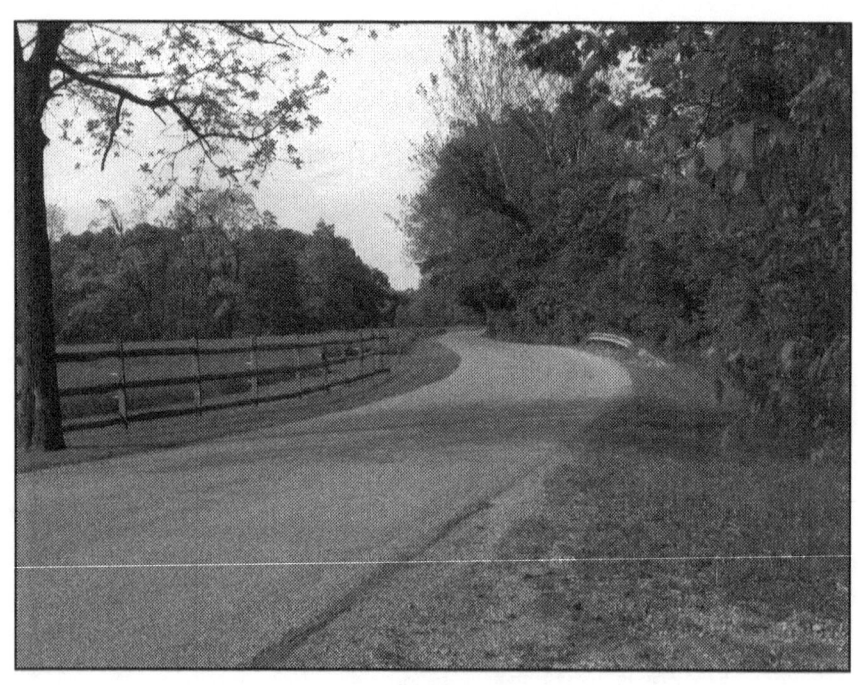

Just a Road
Scene from Moccasin Road - taken by Amy J. Cooper.

Just a...

To some this may be just a road,
   To some place around the bend,
Where things will happen, things will be,
   Perhaps for a postcard to send.

To me it is a favored place,
   That winds through trees and stream.
Far more beauty I ever thought,
   Or I had ever dreamed.

This is more than just a road,
   It's a place of now and olden day,
A way to wind my thoughts to you,
   And bring you, my dream, my way.

...road

Seasons in Circleville

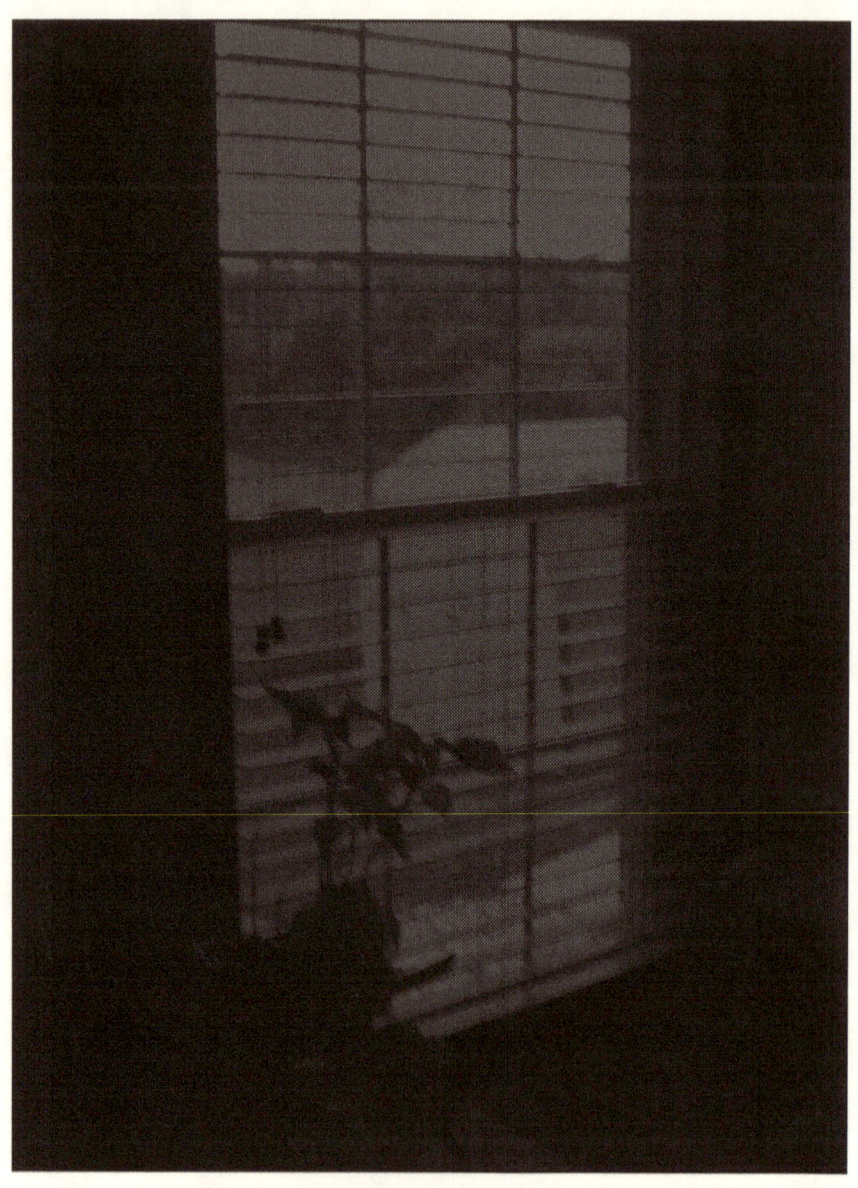

It's 4 a.m. and he must leave for work
Scene from author's home - taken by Amy J. Cooper.

It's 4 a.m. and
he must leave for work

There in the quiet of night
    In the light of the moon
        My world is not right
            For he's left too soon

I hear his feet tread
    Softly on the snow
        I move from my bed
            To the window I go

    I pull back the drapes
        And watch him escape
            Away from the hills
                For a living to make

        And I pray
            For journey safe
                For words unsaid
                    For my love to return
                  To our warm bed

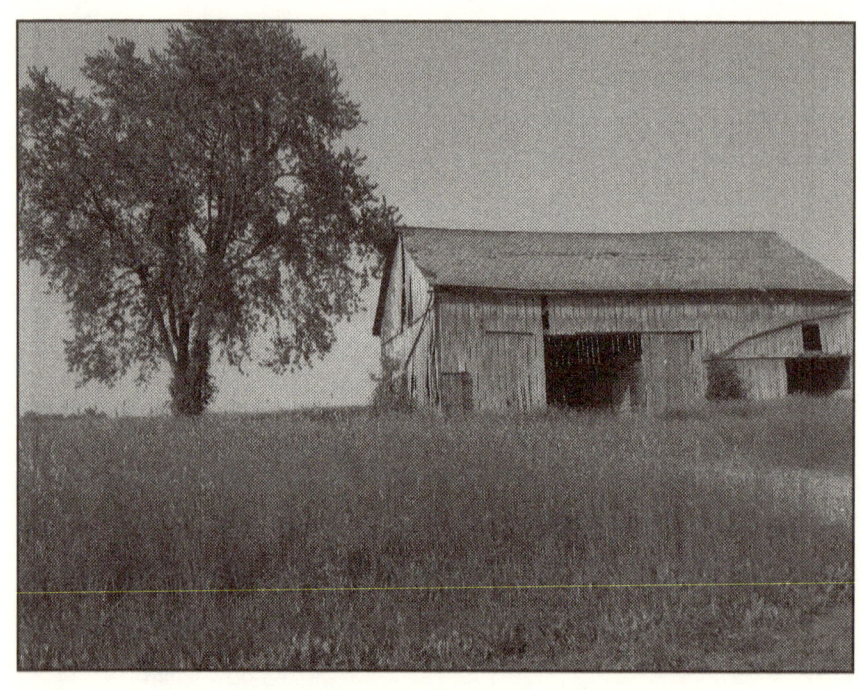

Stopping By a Barn on an Autumn Evening
Scene from Murlette Road - taken by Amy J. Cooper.

Stopping By a Barn
on an Autumn Evening

-With deepest respect and apologies to Robert Frost

Whose barn this is, I think I know.
    His house is in the city though.
        He will not see me stopping here,
            To watch the leaves dancing to and fro.

My lovely dog must think it queer,
    To stop without a drink of water near,
        Between the barn and autumn woods.
            The balmiest evening of the year.

She gives her beautiful tail a shake,
    To ask if there is some mistake.
        The only other sound's the howl,
            Of coyote song down by the lake.

The barn is lovely, amongst the trees,
    But we have moments more like these,
        And much to see before we sleep,
            And much to see before we sleep.

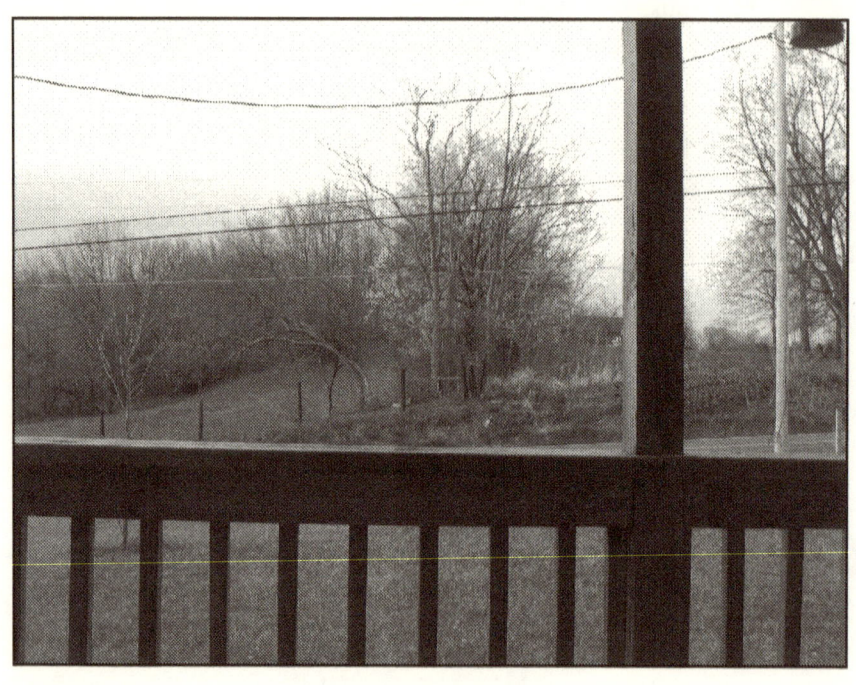

Seasons for the Soul
View from author's home - taken by Amy J. Cooper.

Seasons for the Soul

Winter is the time for me,
       For the love I have to downhill ski.
And, of course, there is no greater thrill,
       Than to go sledding down my very own hill.
Yes, winter is the time for me,
       To set my mind and spirit free.

And yet when the snow turns to rain,
       I find in spring my love's refrain.
For no greater gift will there ever be,
       Than the song of finch for company.
Yes, spring is the time for me,
       To set my mind and spirit free.

Warmer still my heart will grow,
       As summer sun is setting low,
And cricket and owl in lovely song of night,
       Fill me with peace that all is right.
Yes, summer is the time for me,
       To set my mind and spirit free.

And then my heart with color fills,
       With leaves divine as the air chills.
And crisp with pleasure my spirit will dance,
       As the song of autumn my heart enchants.
Yes, autumn is the time for me,
       To set my mind and spirit free.

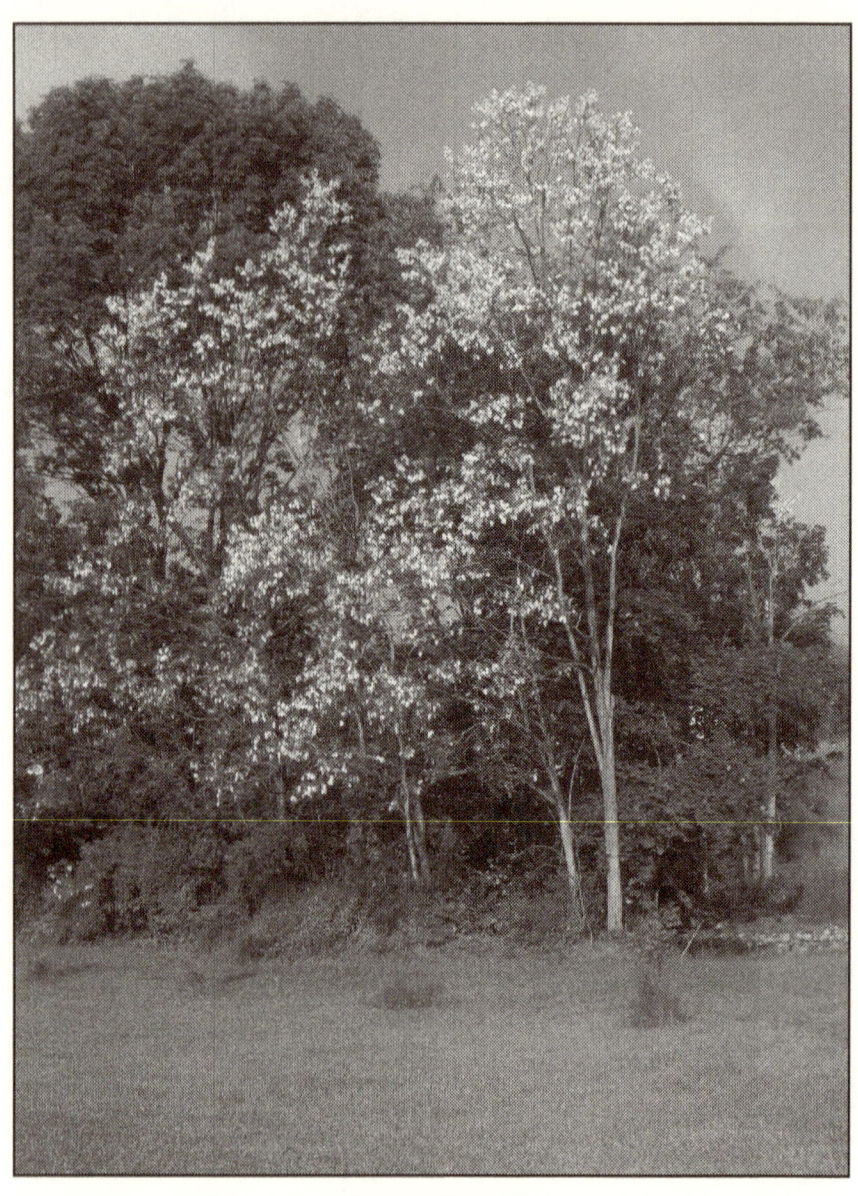

Song of Spring
Scene from author's yard - taken by Amy J. Cooper.

Song of Spring

In the fresh morning dew,
      I cleanse my soul with life anew.
I know not why I feel this way,
      For truly I love the snowy days.

And yet to be free from winter's chill,
      As my eyes gaze over the distant hills,
I feel released, suddenly free,
      My heart sings out with blissful glee.

How thrilled I am that spring is here,
      With scents I smell and songs I hear.
Filled with hope for the plans which I have made,
      For warm spring nights with owl's serenade.

For whilst I love the wintry snow,
      Into the spring my heart will go,
For like a puppet on a string,
      My heart dances to the songs of spring.

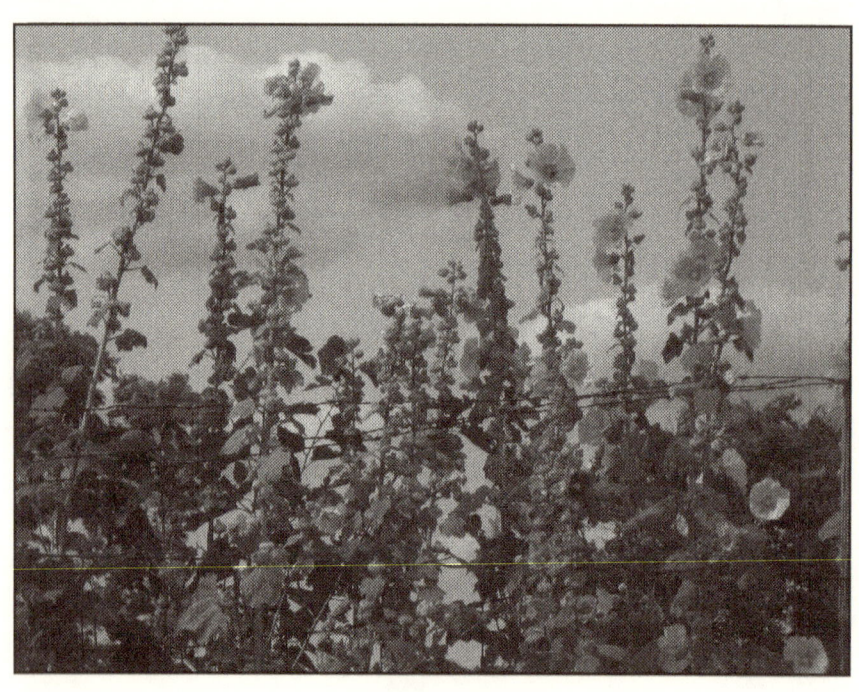

Hollyhocks
Scene from Crites Road, Circleville, Ohio - taken by Amy J. Cooper.

Hollyhocks

Hollyhocks, hollyhocks, all in a row,
    What a lovely display, the gardener has grown.
The colors dance lightly,
    With the kiss of the day,
Towering o'er the fence,
    The hollyhocks sway.

Hollyhocks, hollyhocks, who would have known,
    Your biennial beauty when your seedlings were sown?
The gardener had plotted and came up with a plan,
    But your beauty surpassed it,
With your colors so grand.

Hollyhocks, hollyhocks, how can I say,
    How grateful I am for your gift today?

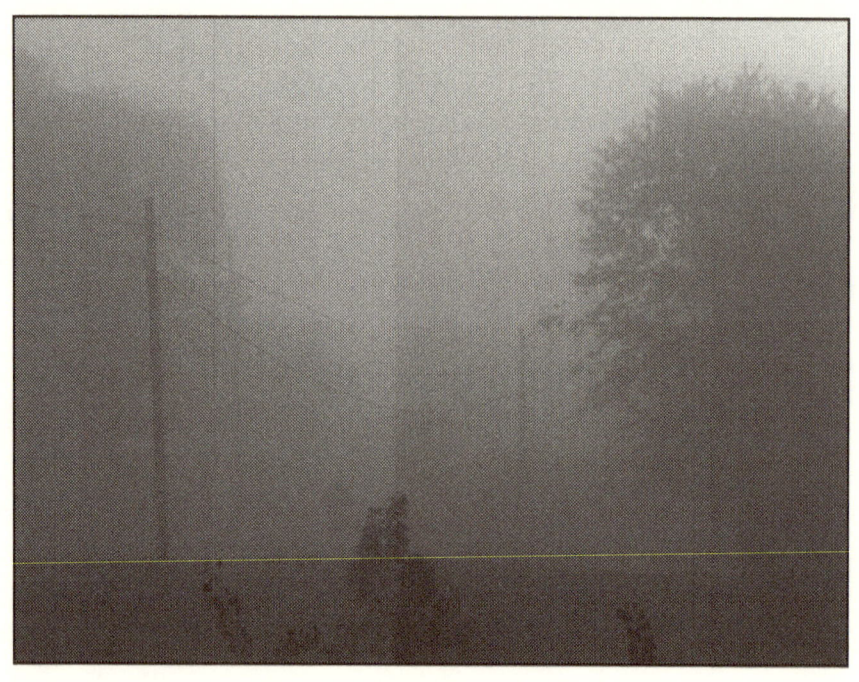

Fog
Scene from author's home - taken by Amy J. Cooper.

Fog

Ever so silently, it carefully creeps,
    Through the hills and the meadows,
        The dense fog seeps.

The great oak and pine,
    Are hidden from view.
        Lost are the houses,
            In the deep, foggy dew.

The crickets cease chirping,
    Quieted song of the owl,
        Through the night they were singing,
            Through the night until now.

On my own front porch,
    Yet in a world I do not know,
        I'm silently wondering,
            Where did familiar things go?

Under fog's blanket,
    My world is concealed.
        Not 'til the warmth of the dawn,
            To again be revealed.

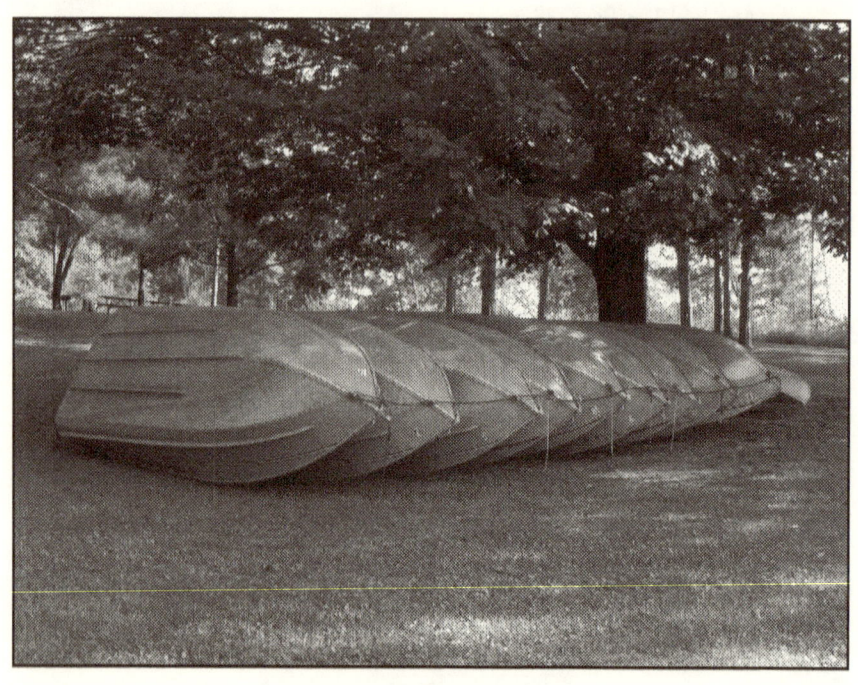

The Boats Will Be Waiting
Scene from Hargus Lake - taken by Amy J. Cooper.

The Boats Will Be Waiting

The lake has grown quiet,
The summer's at end.
The rowboats are tied up.
Winter's 'round the bend.

Echoes of laughter,
Still dance through the trees,
Forever to linger,
In our memories.

Stacked on the shore and locked in chains,
The boats silently stand solemn,
Symbols of summer's refrains.

Through the cold of the winter,
Until spring's blossoms awake,
The boats will be waiting,
For warm summer's lake.

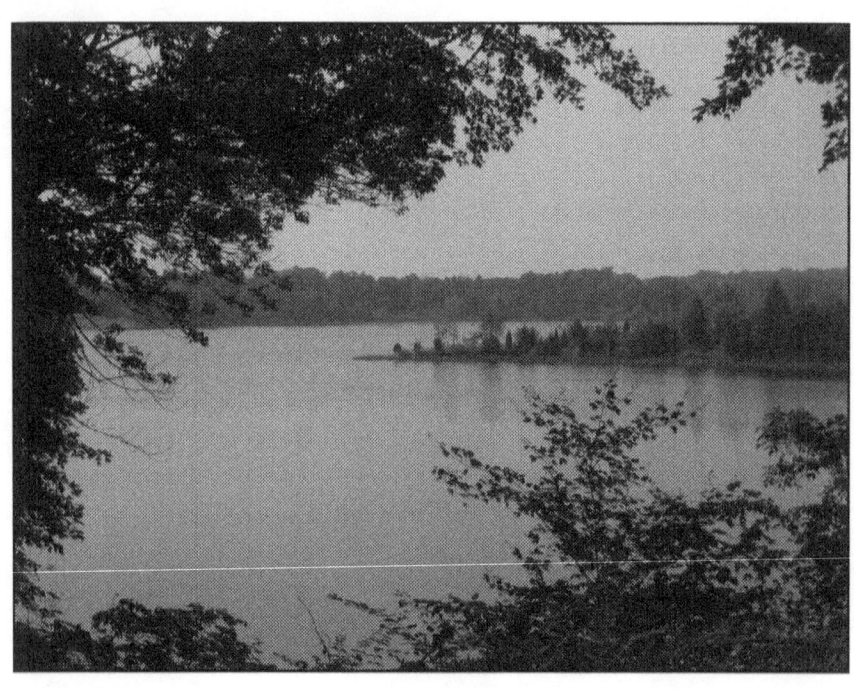

Hargus
Scene from Hargus Lake - taken by Amy J. Cooper.

Hargus

Swiftly, yet silently, I skim the lake;
    Quietly canoeing,
        With the smallest of wake.

Across the Hargus, I paddle,
    With ne'er a sound.
Black-eyed Susans and butterflies,
    On the shore abound.

The warm scents of summer,
    Across the water drift,
Warming my soul with pleasure,
    Cause my spirit to lift.

How could it happen?
    How could it be?
        That this place we call Hargus,
        Is now home to me?

The Hills

    I am in love with the land, this is true. Pickaway County has those unending flat fields where you are certain you can see the end of the earth. Beyond these fields are the hills, the hills of Circleville, and the hills of the surrounding counties, Fairfield, Ross and Hocking. From our home, Gregory and I can see them all. They have stirred my soul. They have crept into my dreams, into my heart and consumed my mind. No matter where else I may live, these hills will always haunt me.

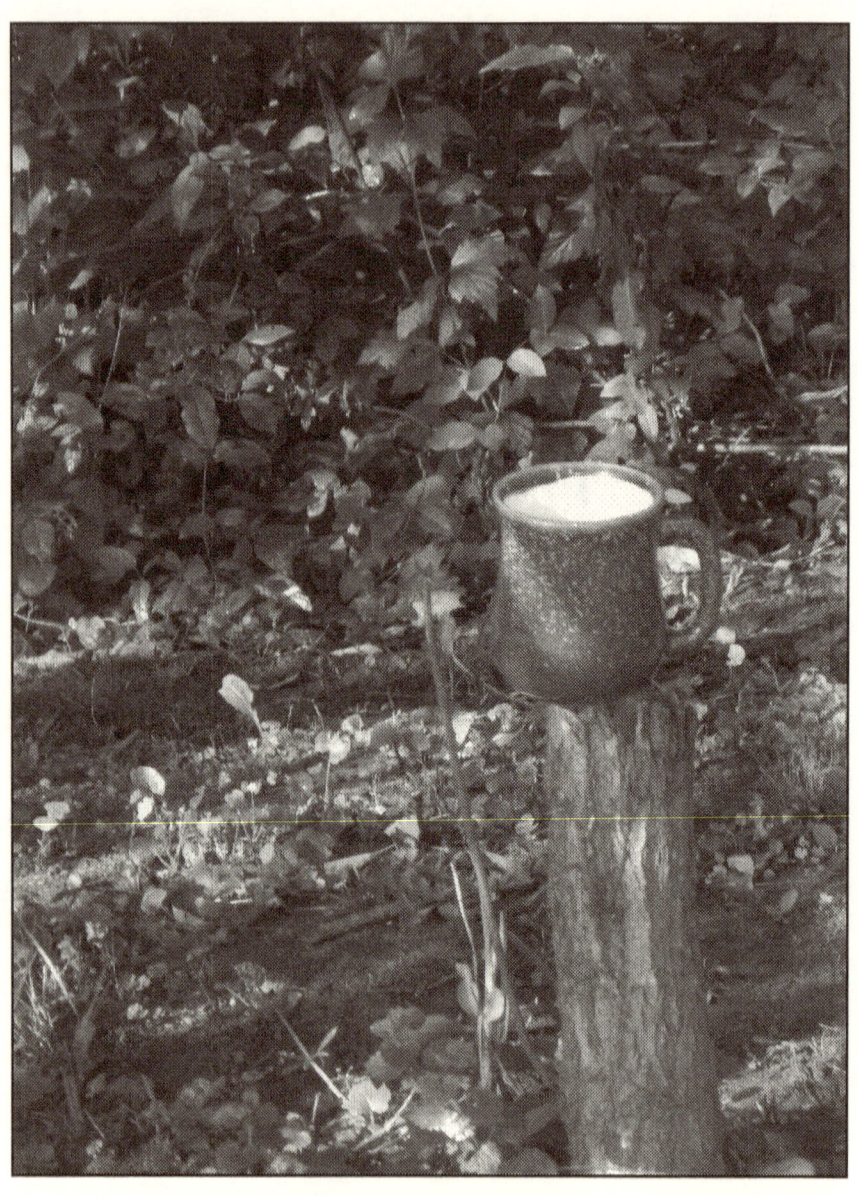

Running Late for Work
Scene from author's backyard - taken by Amy J. Cooper.

Running Late for Work...

I believe I will be late again.
   Yes, I believe that is true.
For I'm watching the sun slowly rise,
   To paint the sky clear blue.

Yes, I may be late for work today.
   For when the fog is in the air,
How can I turn my gaze away?
   I just sip my coffee and off I stare.

I cannot yet begin the day,
   When the fog is in the trees,
And the sun has yet to clear the way,
   For the early morning breeze.

Yes, yes, I'm sure of it as I take another sip,
   I find my coffee has grown cold,
While my mind went on a trip.

There is some place I am supposed to be,
   But they'll understand, I'm sure they'll see,
That there really is no other way,
   To greet the world and start my day,
Than to look out over the stream and trees,
   And watch the hills fill with morning breeze.

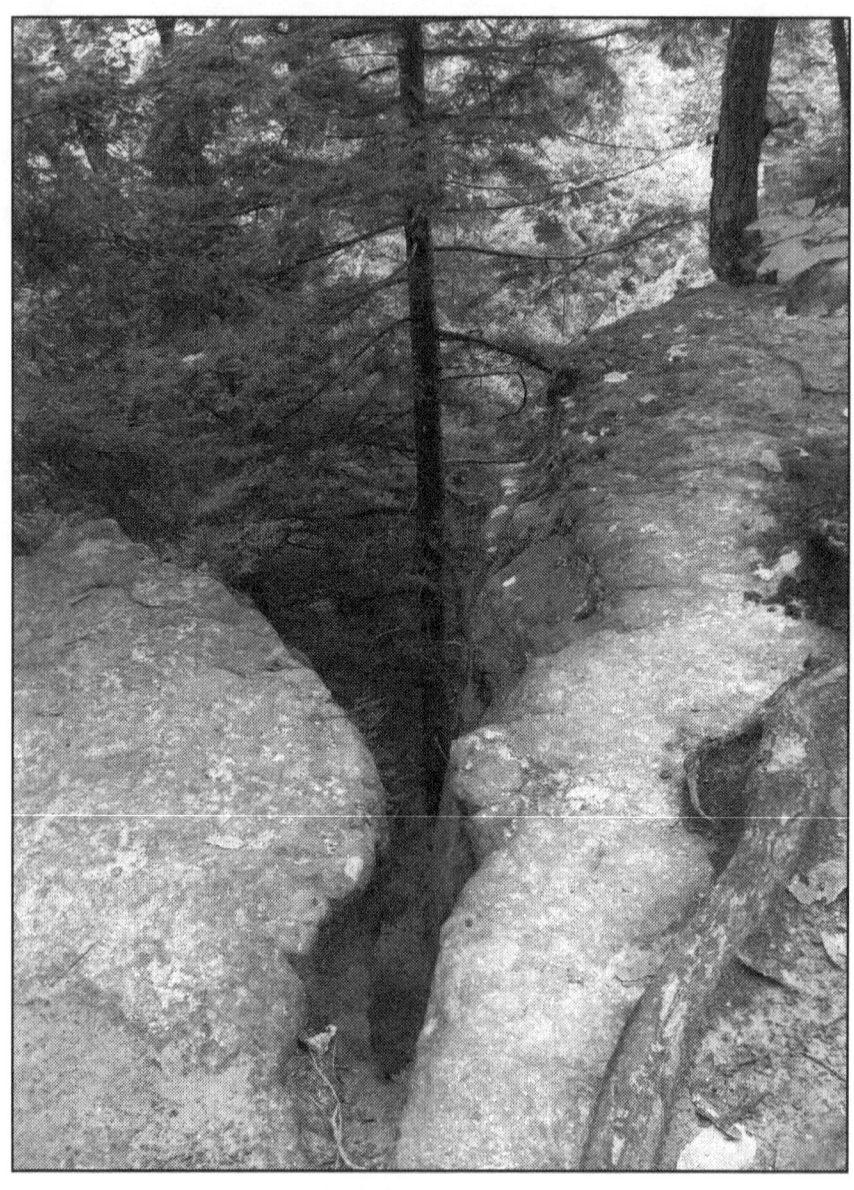

Your Right to Choose
Scene from the Rock House in the Hocking Hills – taken by Amy J. Cooper.

Your Right to Choose

Standing on the edge of a cliff,
      Staring down into the hills deep and green,
For all my life I've never known,
      And such a lovely sight, I've never seen.

A strike of a match off to my left,
      And my thoughts stray from the scene divine,
As you take a puff and move your feet,
      First one, then the other, closer to mine.

Your lungs are free and filled with air,
      Mine are tight and damaged by disease.
You blow your smoke and I gasp with despair,
      For any moment my lungs, my life, may cease.

It is your right to smoke, this I know,
      For who am I to ask that you go,
Far from my hills, far from my trees,
      Take away this pain floating in the breeze.

The fear is strong but not for my death,
      I've always known each may be my last breath,
But rather I fear your right to choose,
      Who should win and who should lose.
With those ashes you flicker, who will you kill,
      Will it be me, or my lovely green hills?

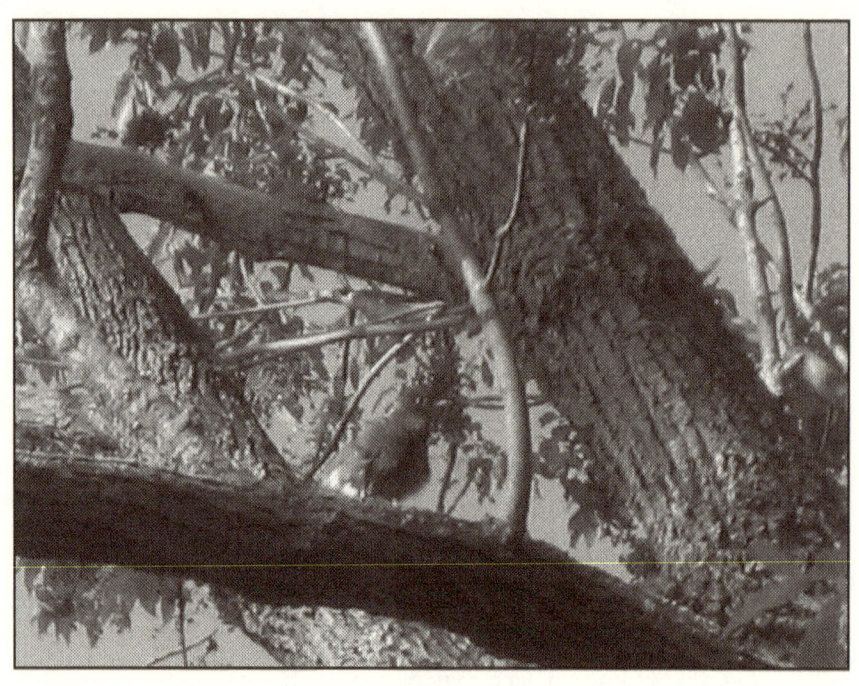

Music
Scene from author's backyard - taken by Amy J. Cooper.

Music

It's in the birds as in the trees they land,
It's in the song of the owl as it sings to "who."
It's in my heart as you take my hand,
The hills are alive with my love for you.

You have my heart, and the hills my soul.
Nothing left, I've been consumed whole,
By nature's music and the spring air,
That fills the hills with song so rare.

The song of love fills the night,
As clouds slowly ease across the sky,
The moon is revealed and in the glow of its light,
I know in my heart that, at last, my world is right.

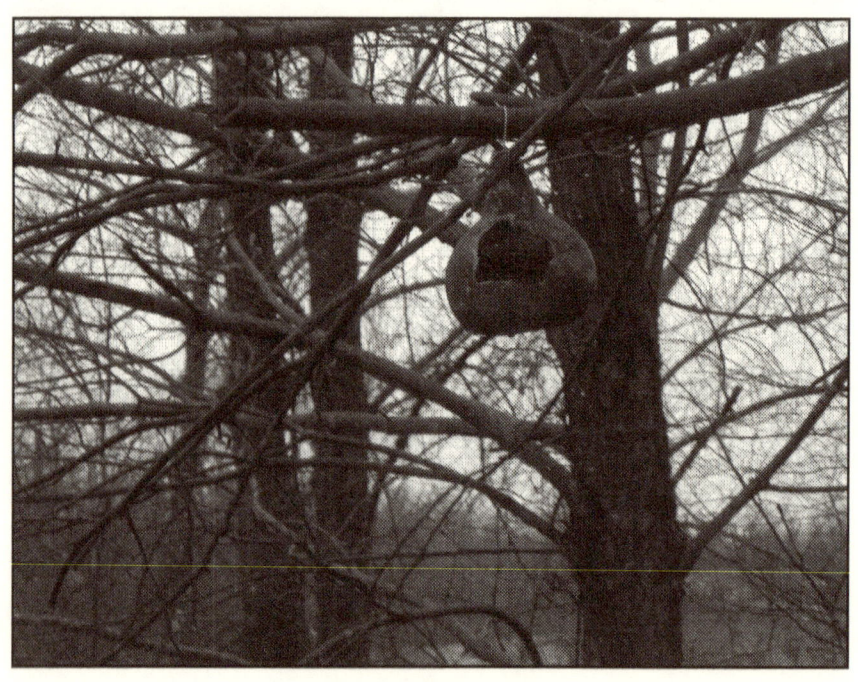

You are Home to Me
Scene from author's backyard - taken by Amy J. Cooper.

You are Home to Me

(For Marlo and Julie)

Wherever you are, that is where I will be.
For wherever you'll be, will be home to me.

You are the place I come to,
At the end of the day.
You bring me peace and comfort,
Somehow you know the way.

It is in your beautiful hand,
As you softly hold mine.
Our love forever stands still,
In a moment in time.

It is in your warm and lovely smile,
That fills my heart all the while,
I am away from you in the long of day.
No words are spoken, and yet I hear you say,
That I am home.

A home can be found in any place,
For it is deep in the heart,
Filled with love's giving grace.
And wherever you go, my love,
Wherever you roam,
'Tis there you will find me,
For you are my home.

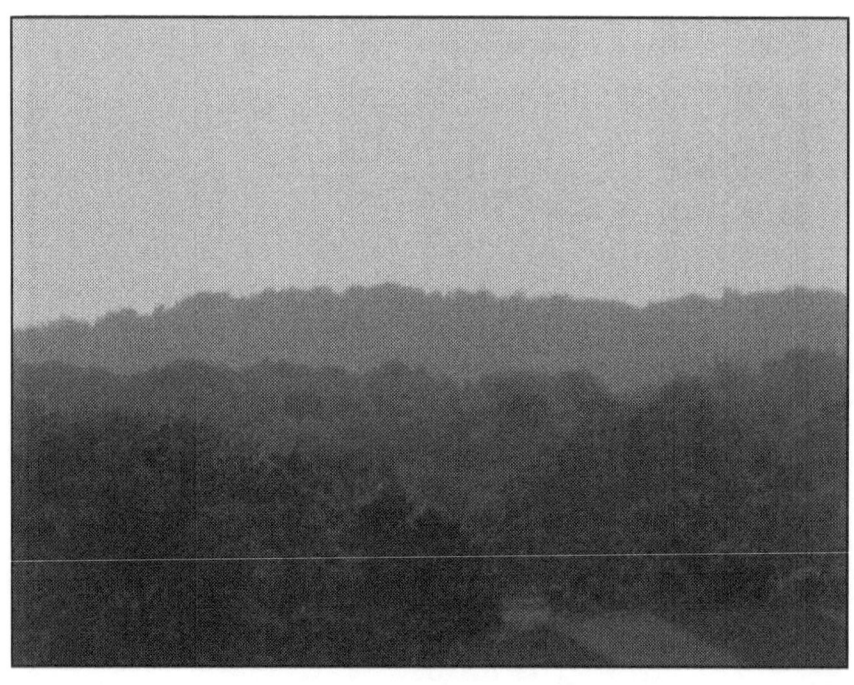

Coming Home
Scene from Tarlton Road - taken by Amy J. Cooper.

Coming Home

For oft when on this road I drive,
   My heart beats fast and I come alive,
When the view of rolling hills come into sight,
   As if with wings, my soul takes flight.

Suddenly my being is filled with glee,
   For never did I think I'd see,
On my road home, such lines of trees,
   To color the hills who sing to me.

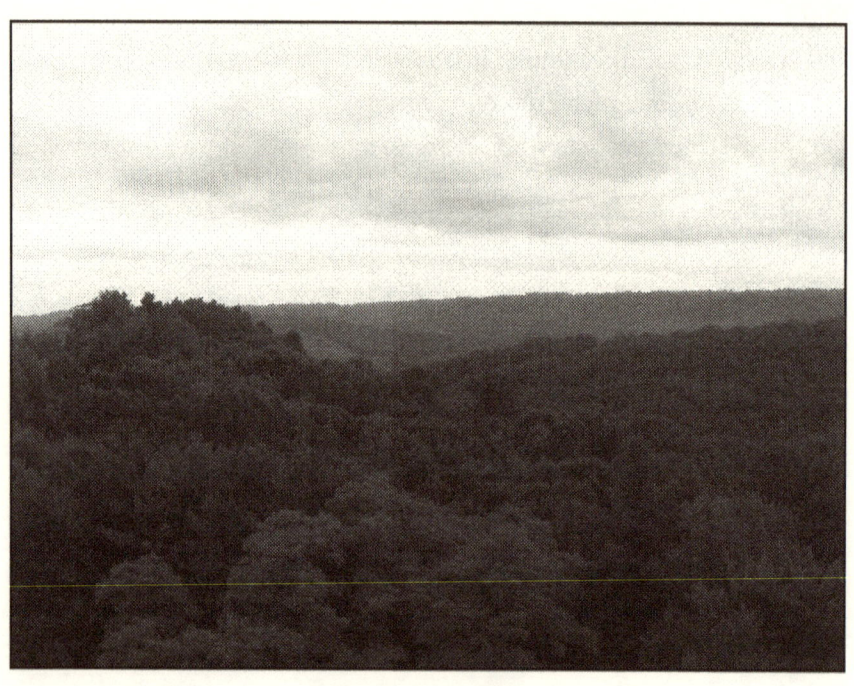

Out in the Rain
Scene from Thompson Ridge Road (the Hocking Hills) -
taken by Amy J. Cooper.

Out in the Rain
(the Hocking Hills)

*(Inspired by Circleville's The House Band performing
the song Out in the Rain written by Julie Miller.)*

The Hocking Hills are calling,
      Calling me by name,
When I first saw them,
      I knew I'd not be the same.

Off into the distance,
      My heart is set aflight,
Over the trees and hillsides,
      Into the deep of night.

In the deep green sea of forest,
      Are secrets left untold.
In the infinite hills and valleys,
      Are stories of my soul.

Out in the rain is where you'll find me,
      Talking to the trees,
My eyes gazing skyward,
      My face turned toward the breeze.

As I drink the drops of rain,
      In the hills of green I roam,
The place I have been seeking,
      The place to call my home.

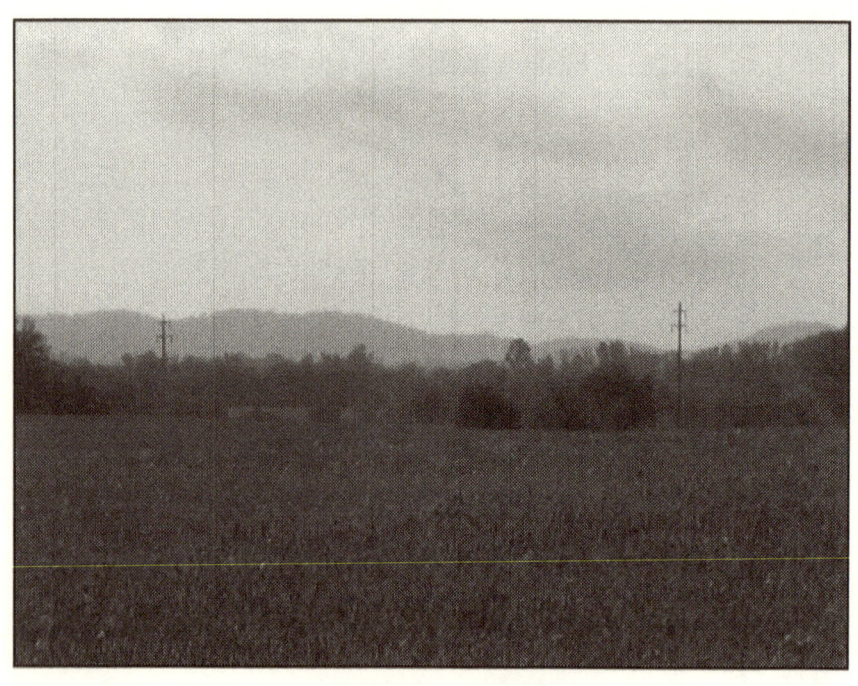

The Hills of Chillicothe
Scene from Tarlton Road, Circleville, Ohio - taken by Amy J. Cooper.

The Hills of Chillicothe

Every morning you rise to greet me,
As I travel into town.
You roll along the byway,
And fill my heart with song.

I learned quickly to respect you.
Your hills are steep to climb.
The view from top Mount Sugarloaf,
Is sheer pleasure made divine.

Down to the streets below,
Roll the hills of Chillicothe.
Around the bend, up Western Ave.,
Waving the streets of the city.

Over the fields the hills roll on,
To the deep woods not far away,
Where history of Tecumseh,
Transcends us from this day.

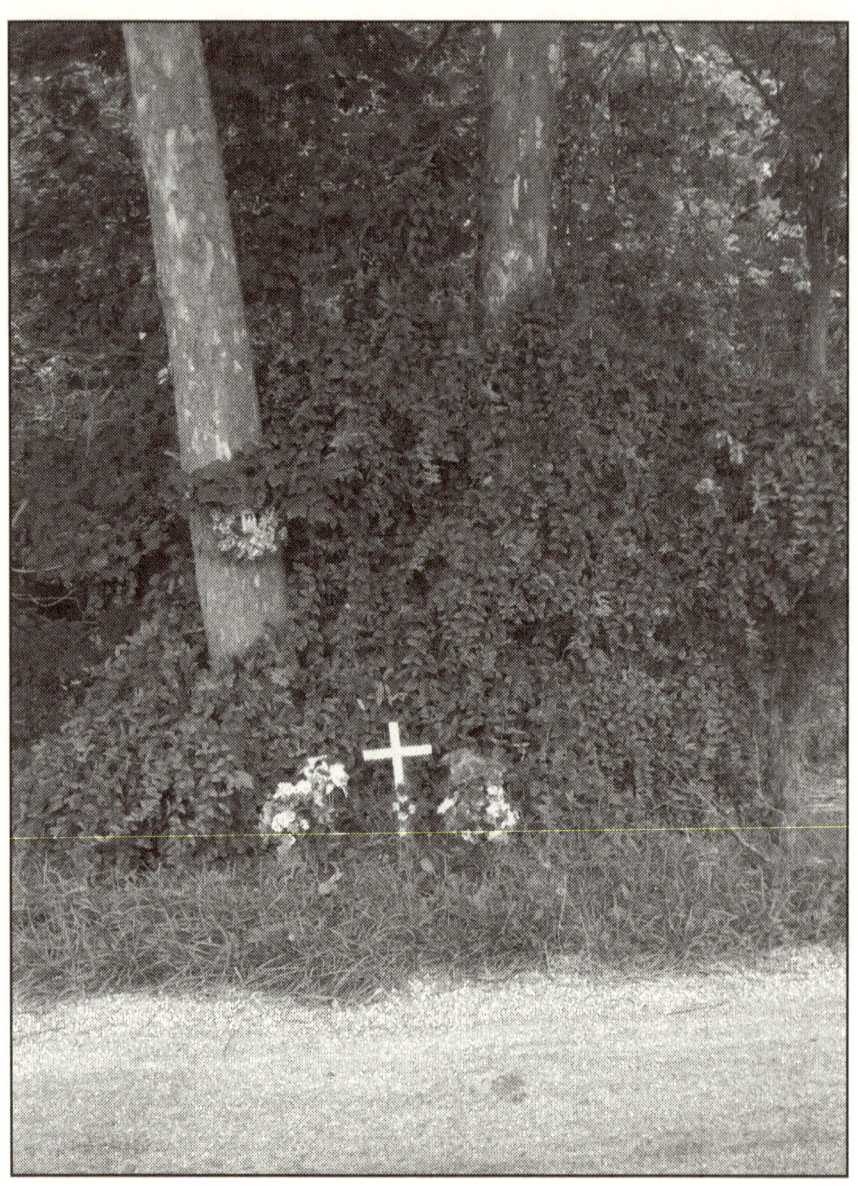

Road Signs
Scene from Moccasin Road - taken by Amy J. Cooper.

Road Signs

I know not who you were,
      Or how many lives you touched.
But I see from the road signs,
      They miss you very much.

I know not what had happened,
      On that tragic day.
But I'm sure it was too sudden,
      That you were taken away.

Nearly never does a day go by,
      That I don't see the signs,
Left to honor a cherished memory,
      For those who are left behind.

...Of Circleville

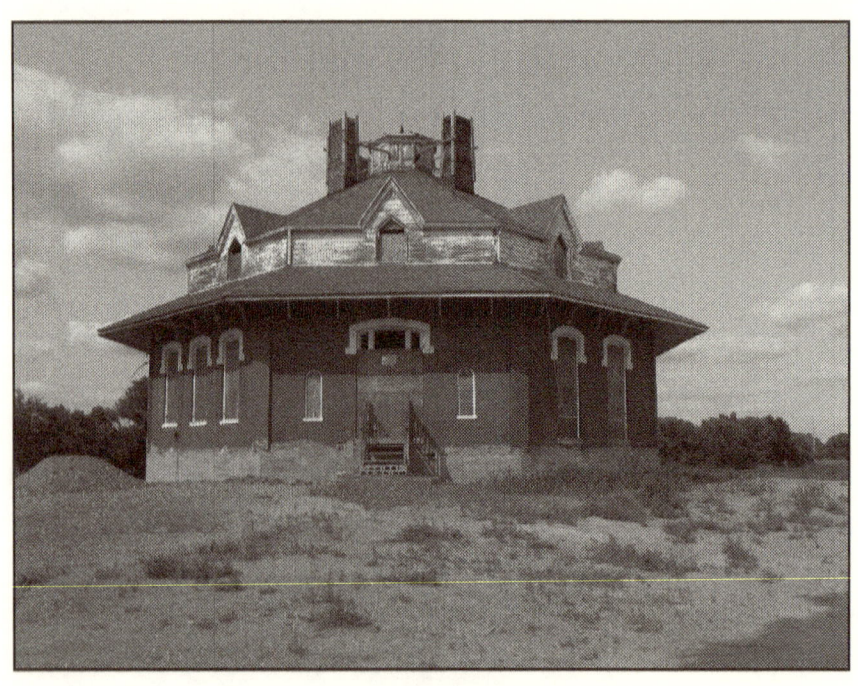

The Octagon
Scene from Crites Road (off of Route 23),
Circleville, Ohio - taken by Amy J. Cooper.

The Octagon

So many sides to every story,
        So many tales of life and glory.
You, my friend, have sides of eight.
        And yet unknown remains your fate.

The side, the story, of your creation,
        Is of architect rare and family elation.
You stood so grand, unique and erect.
        Who knew the lives you would effect?

Beside the barn, out in the field,
        Who ever thought you'd need to yield?
Since 1855 you took your stand,
        Your piece of history on your piece of land.

To find one day you would be told,
        The land 'neath your feet had been sold.
Demolition soon to be your fate,
        Razing the home with walls of eight.

And just as the end was drawing nigh,
        A small gathering occurred in a tavern nearby.
"We must save the Octagon!" they cried in despair,
        And the plan that was formed was clever and rare.

Another piece of the land, small but would do,
        Was granted for moving the Octagon to.
Ever slowly and gently she moved to new land.
        And there oh, so elegant the Octagon stands.

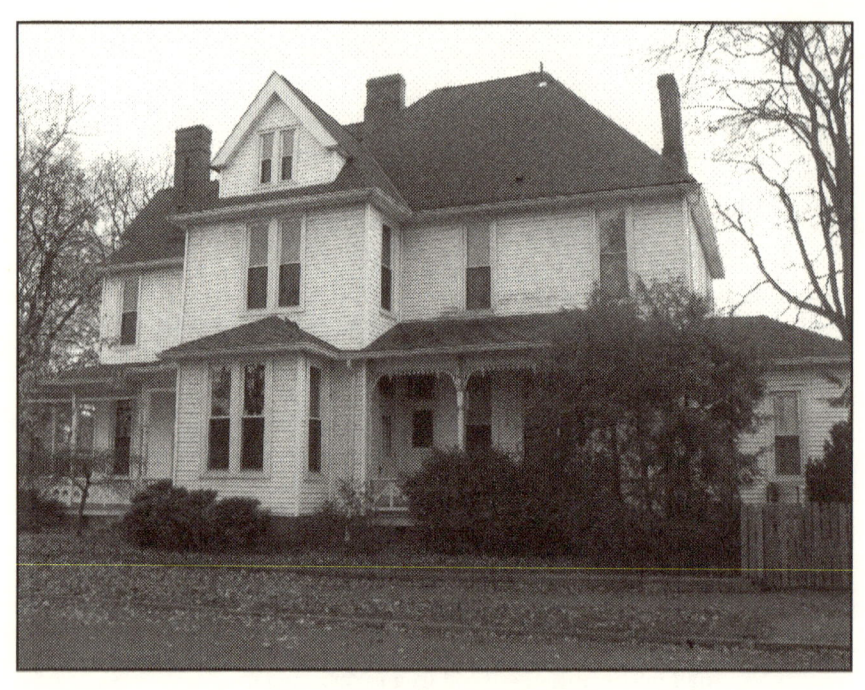

The Musician and His Wife
Scene from Circleville, Ohio - taken by Amy J. Cooper.

The Musician and His Wife

A musician lives here,
    With his wife divine,
        They have two lovely children,
            And a dog I wish was mine.

With a lovely, sweet smile,
    She lights up the night.
        With a song so soulful,
            He sets the spirit aflight.

The children on journeys to further their minds,
    Come home through the seasons,
        The family a circle,
            The love that binds.

Sometimes in the evening,
    When days' work is done,
        We sit in their kitchen,
            And let our minds roam.

We take trips to the oceans,
    And lands far away,
        But never far from our hills,
            Have we yet to stray.

We talk about music,
    And sometimes he sings.
        As she watches him lovingly,
            I know there is no better thing,
    Than to have friends such as these,
        Who bring music to our minds, our souls,
            And play our heart strings.

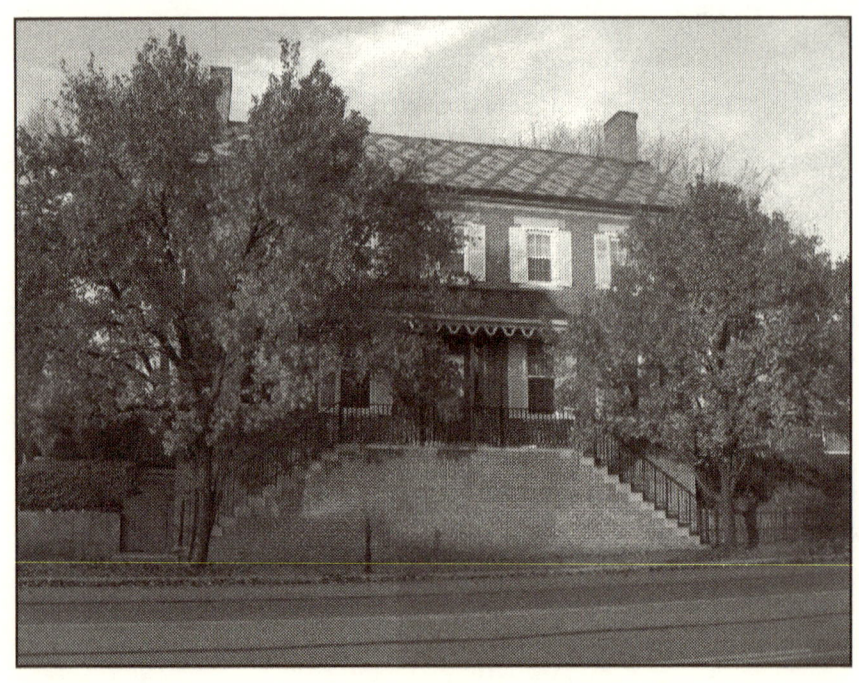

George
Scene from Circleville, Ohio - taken by Amy J. Cooper.

George

The iron pony with ring still stands,
    Where horses once were tethered.
        Two sets of stairs ascend,
            To heavy door old and weathered.

Beyond the door the spirits dwell,
    Amazing eyes gaze upon you, she casts a spell.
        He's grand and seems of another time.
            They smile at you and you feel your heart unwind.

As pleasant and lovely as these spirits be,
    They are of the living, we can touch and see.
        There is yet another dwells in this house of old.
            His name is George, so I've been told.

His time on earth has long passed by,
    Still his spirit opens doors with heavy sighs.
        Yes, a family lives here, there are three,
            All fine spirits, though only two you can see.

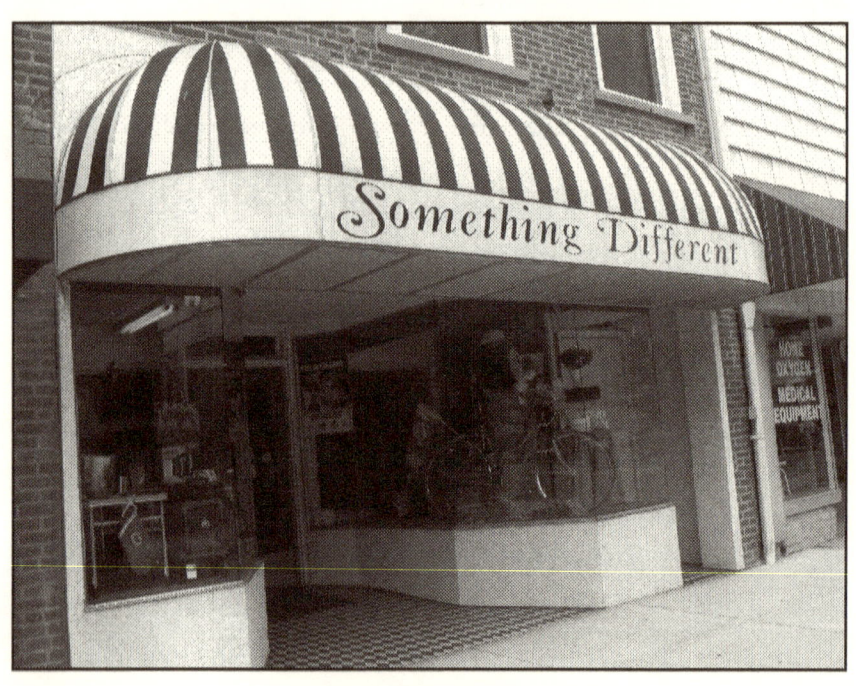

Something Different
Scene from Main Street, Circleville, Ohio - taken by Amy J. Cooper.

Something Different

All things unique and rare,
That you cannot find anywhere,
Are here beyond this glass door,
Such treasures as you've not seen before.

Something Different, something new,
Something for me and something for you.

Life-like dolls sit on the shelves.
When no one is looking,
They help themselves,
To smell a candle or read a book.
C'mon inside and take a look.

OSU fanware such as you've never seen.
You can tell the fanatic by how their eyes gleam.
With joy they will hold a banner in hand,
And immediately transport to the Buckeyes' grandstand.

For those of us not into the sport,
There are candles and jewelry and things of all sorts.
If we ask the dolls nicely, they'll give us a look,
Let us read from the pages of the Wicked Dreams book.

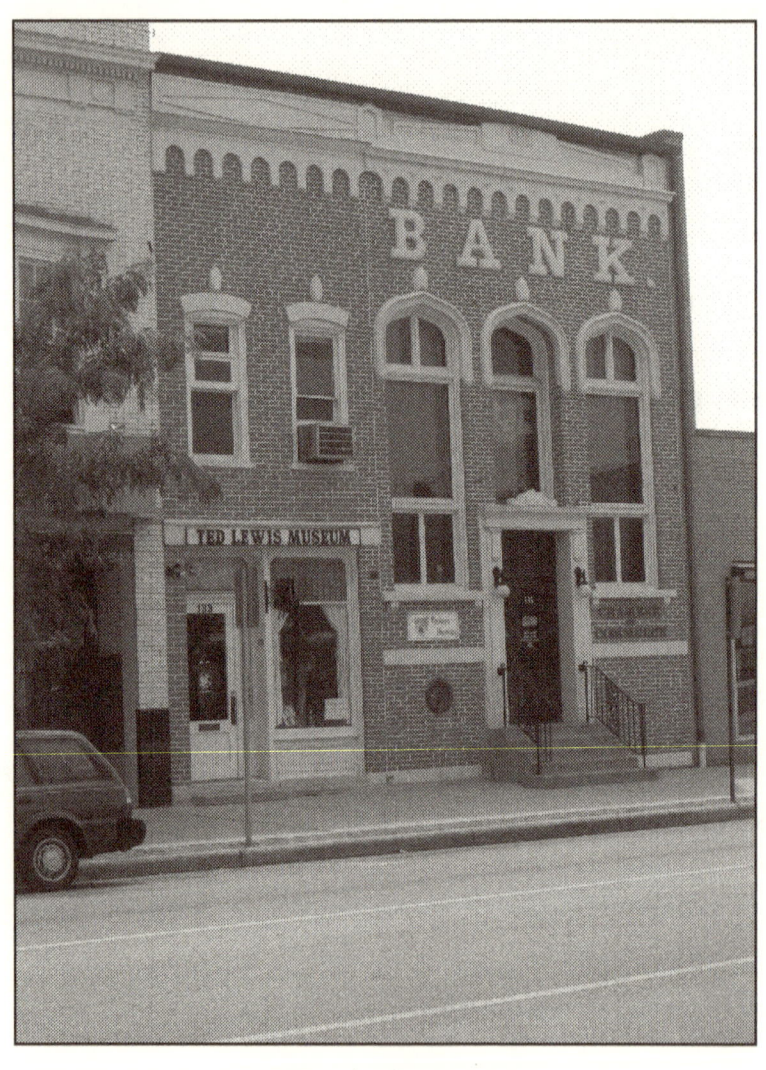

Is Everybody Happy?
Scene from Main Street, Circleville, Ohio - taken by Amy J. Cooper.

Is Everybody Happy?

Go down to the corner,
> And a little further past,
If you go on a Friday,
> A friendly voice will ask,
"Is everybody happy?"
> And you cannot help but be,
For you're at the Ted Lewis Museum,
> A place of memories.

In a case of wood and glass,
> His worn top hat sits.
You want to take it out and see,
> If on your head it fits.

The photos are soft memories,
> Of days of song and dance.
You feel you've stepped back in time,
> Your mind is in a trance.

The curtain drawn, you've seen the show,
> Reluctantly, it's time to go.
But before he will set you free,
> Again he'll ask "Is everybody happy?"

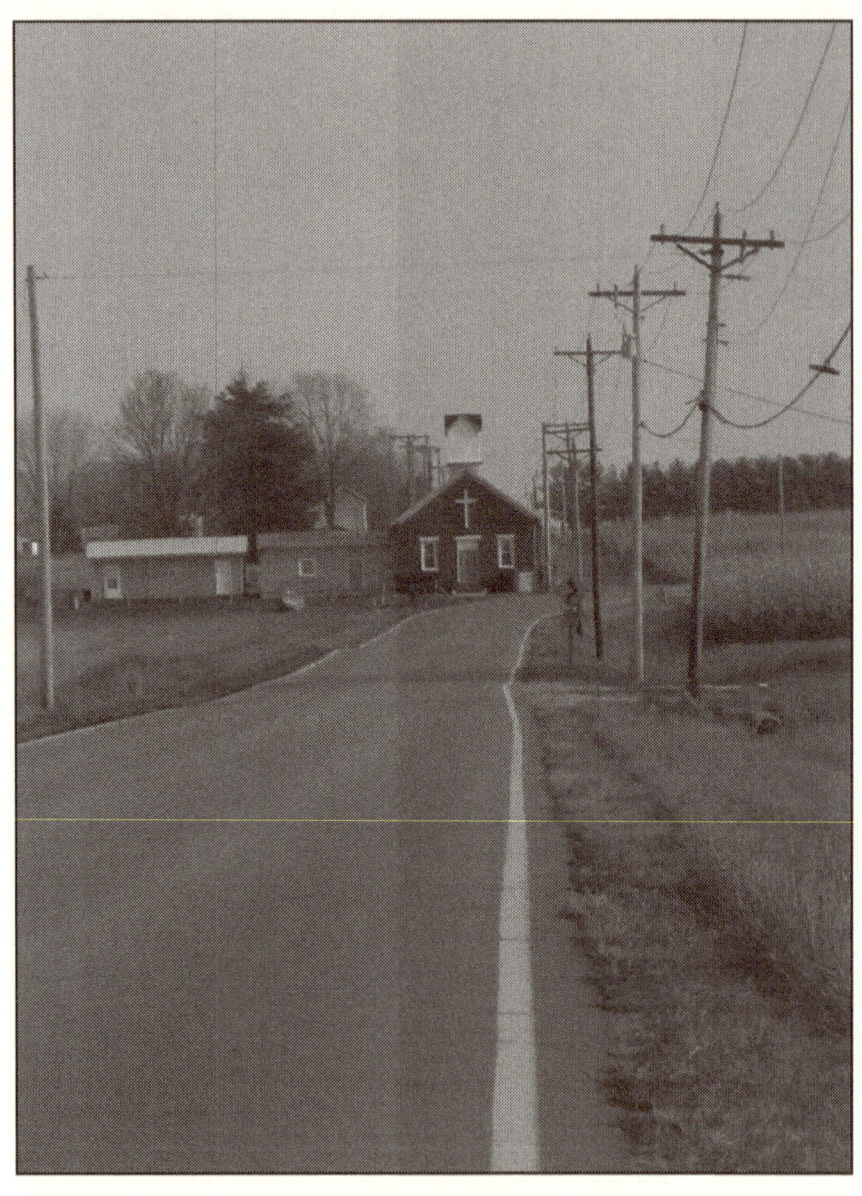

He is Unavoidable
Scene from Tarlton Road, Pickaway County, Ohio - taken by Amy J. Cooper.

He is Unavoidable

It is not an illusion,
    It is as it should be,
The church that stands before you,
    In the middle of the road it seems.

You fear the road will take you,
    Straight through its narrow aisle,
And up to the pulpit.
    Your heart beats faster all the while.

Just as you gasp, "Will this be the end?"
    The road suddenly changes,
And wraps around the bend.

You've narrowly escaped, you believe,
    From tragic accident.
But how is it that you conceive,
    That your days are chosen spent?

For true as this church in the midst of the road,
    God is everywhere and carries your load.
You may think you'll curve around Him,
    But in the rearview mirror you'll see,
He's the unavoidable and for all eternity.

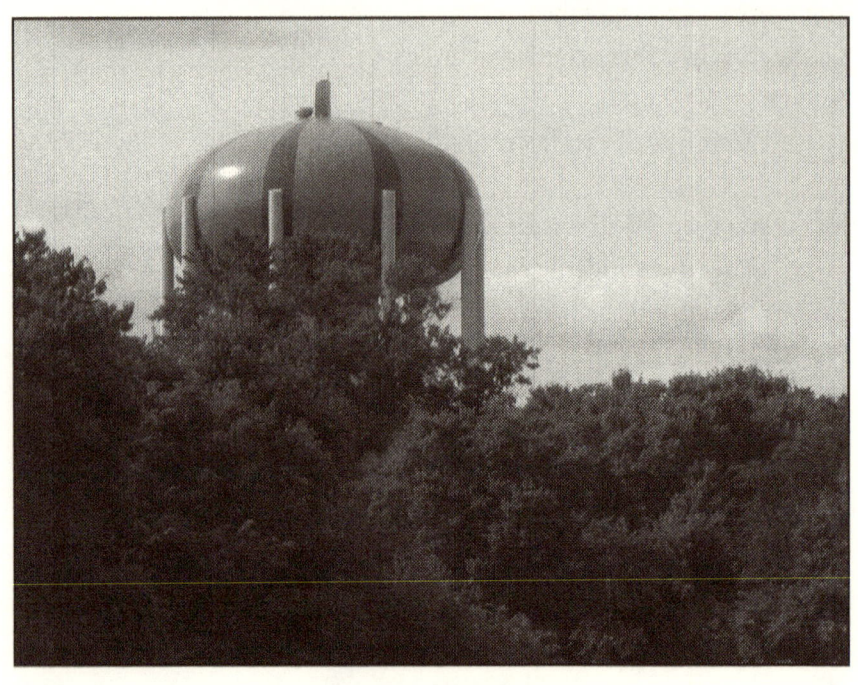

The Pumpkin of Pickaway
Scene from Crites Road (off of Route 23), Circleville, Ohio -
taken by Amy J. Cooper.

The Pumpkin of Pickaway

I am the King of Gourds,
     Rising above the trees,
The greatest pumpkin of all,
     Far distances I see.

I stand guard on this tower,
     Looking over the hills,
Protecting my kingdom,
     Known as Circleville.

I stand guard through the day time,
     And into the night,
Through the quiet of midnight,
     'Til dawn's early light.

A permanent fixture,
     Of the city's skyline,
I'm the Pumpkin of Pickaway.
     I'm here for all time.

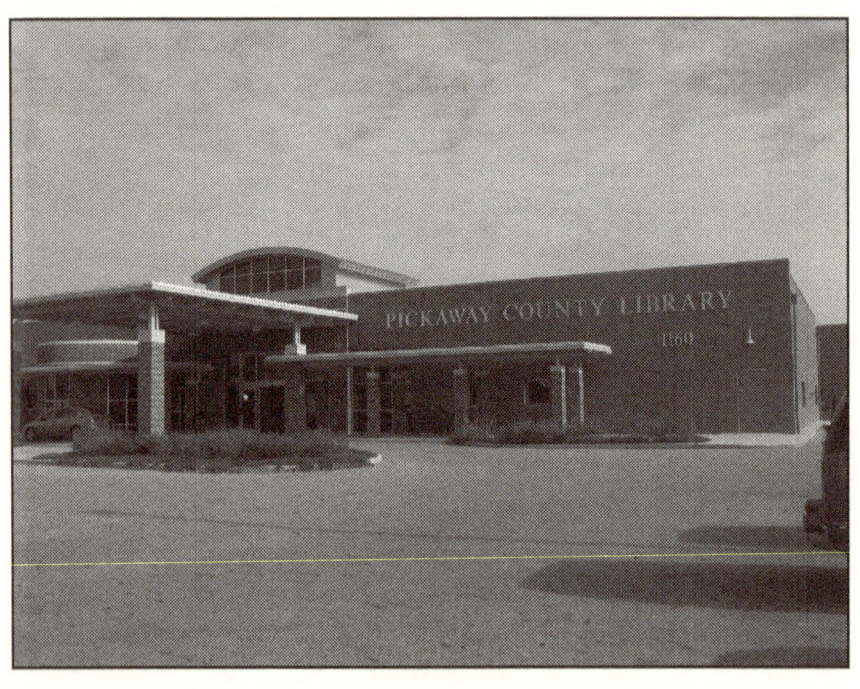

The Library
Scene from North Court Street, Circleville, Ohio - taken by Amy J. Cooper.

The Library

Once you step inside the door,
    You'll find history, biographies,
        Mysteries and more.

Once you lift a book from the shelf,
    You'll lose yourself,
        It can't be helped.

It really isn't very hard.
    Just sign up for a library card.

You will travel the world,
    All in one day.
Yet, here in Circleville,
    Is where you'll stay.

Your feet planted,
    On the library floor,
Your spirits will rise,
    Your mind will soar.

If you can steal your eyes,
    Away from a book,
You'll see there's more in store,
    Just take a look.

Sometimes, someone will come to speak,
    On writing or of places unknown.
And sometimes during the mid of week,
    You'll find a movie is being shown.

Oh, the library is the place to be,
    To set the mind and spirit free.

The Love of
God's Creatures

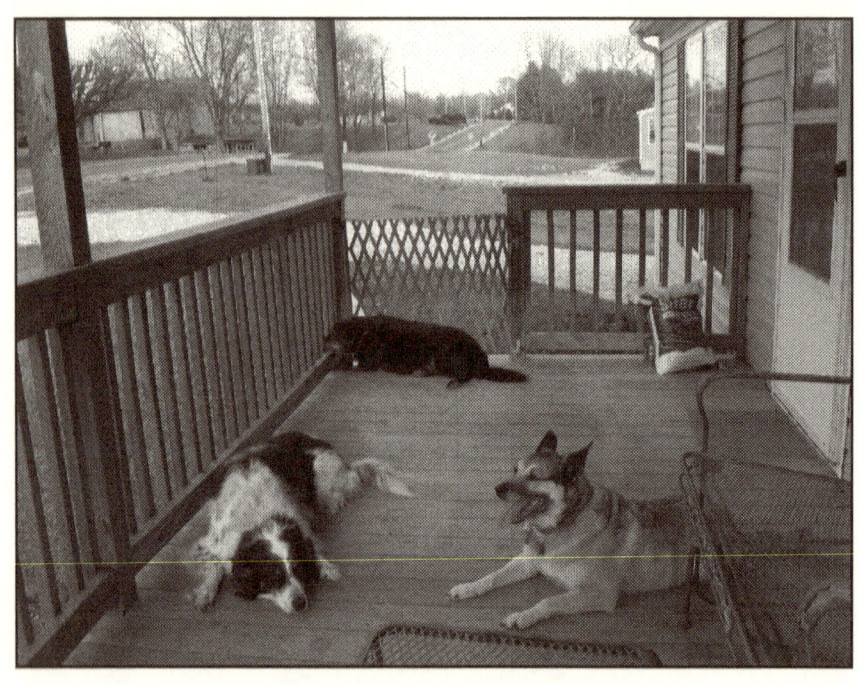

Three Fine Dogs
Scene from the author's home - taken by Amy J. Cooper.

Three Fine Dogs

Three fine dogs live here,
      For it is indeed their fate,
To care for their keepers,
      'Till they stand at Heaven's gate.

Yes, three fine dogs live in this house in the hills.
      They find joy in every moment,
           Little things bring them thrills.

When the horse rides by,
      Or the tractor Deere green,
You'd think no greater thing could be,
      No greater thing they've seen.

Running from room to room,
      Onto the porch of wood,
They bark and grunt and wonder,
      If they really even should.

Yet excitement takes the moment,
      All thoughts of calm are lost,
For now comes the Amish buggy,
      They bark and give their heads a toss.

They carry on through the end of day,
      It matters not what I might say,
For the three fine dogs who live here,
      Will do as they please come what may.

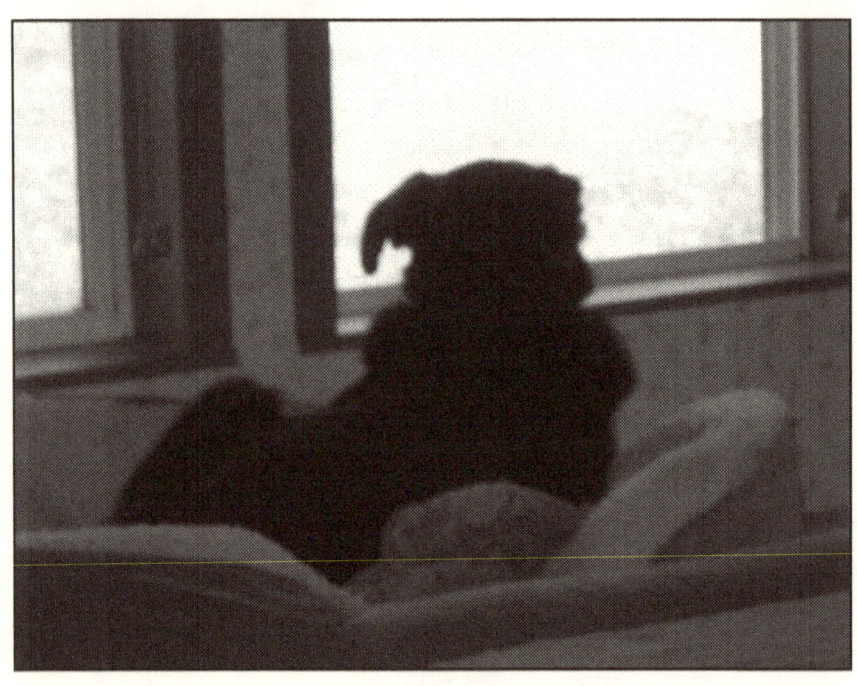

My Window
Jude in his favorite place - taken by Amy J. Cooper.

My Window

(In loving memory and honor of my beloved Jude who passed away during the writing of The Hills of Circleville. I will always love you and hold you near, my big old bear.)

My window is my favorite place,
       To contemplate the human race.
How Blessed to have it be my fate,
       That I should be here on this date,
This day when all the world goes by,
       To touch my heart as I breathe a sigh.

For once when in my life before,
       The hunger made me ignore,
The beauty in the world around,
       The love that would know no bounds.

For out my window, I sit and stare,
       And smell summer scent floating in the air.
And as I gaze out my favorite window,
       I am filled with love and this I know,
That God loves us all in His way,
       For he gave me this window to enjoy this day.

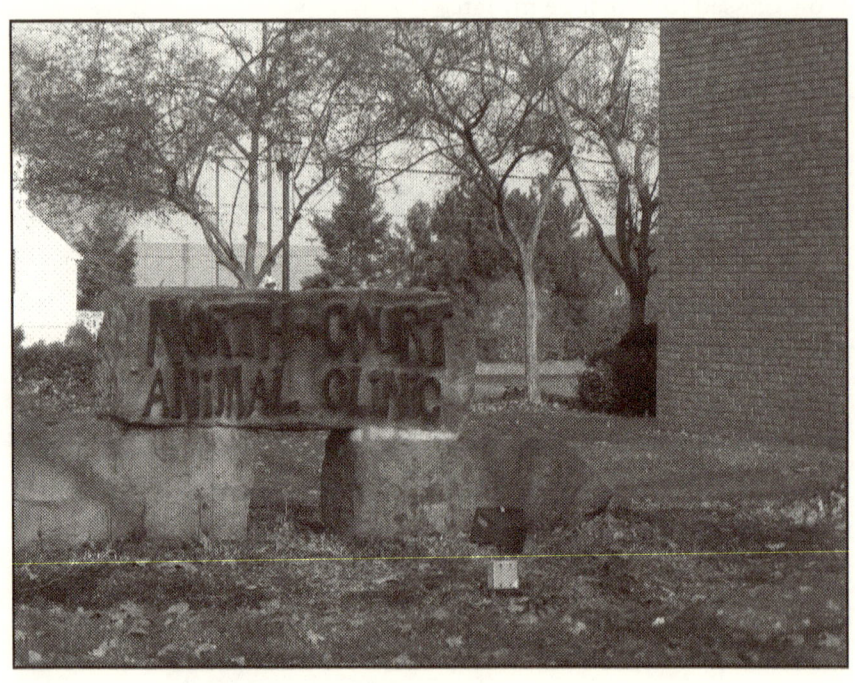

The Caregivers (North Court Animal Clinic)
Scene from Circleville, Ohio - taken by Amy J. Cooper.

The Caregivers

Go through these doors,
       And you'll find inside,
The knowledge and wisdom,
       Of caregivers kind.

The stories are varied,
       So many to tell.
I'll share some with you,
       If you'll sit for a spell.

The devotion of dog,
       Companionship of cat,
The heart's love songs,
       The love that lasts.

Beyond these doors,
       Are stories of hope,
And dignified passings,
       And prayers to help cope.

Beyond these doors,
       The gifts are given,
For those passed on,
       And those left living.

Beyond these doors,
       You'll find wellness of spirit,
Of hope for the future,
       Because these caregivers are in it.

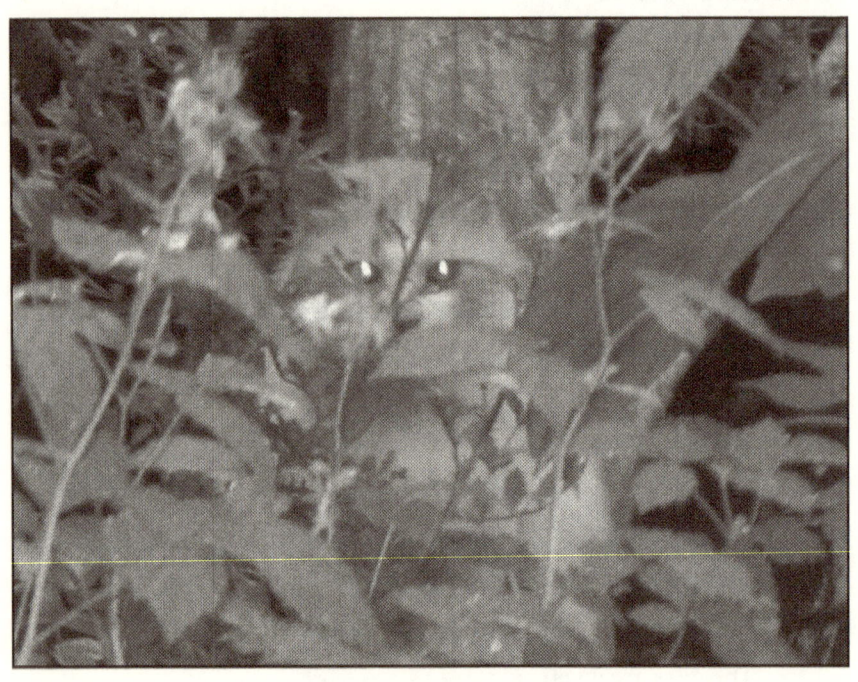

Unexpected Encounter
Scene from the author's yard - taken by Amy J. Cooper.

Unexpected Encounter

I didn't expect to see you.
>> You caught me by surprise.
Suddenly I was captivated,
>> And lost within your eyes.

You sat there oh, so quietly,
>> You scarcely made a move,
Waiting ever so patiently,
>> To see what I would do.

And I, well, I did the same,
>> For you appeared so wild,
Yet sat there oh, so tame,
>> And quiet all the while.

After several moments passed,
>> With ne'er a word spoken,
We parted on our separate ways,
>> With ne'er the silence broken.

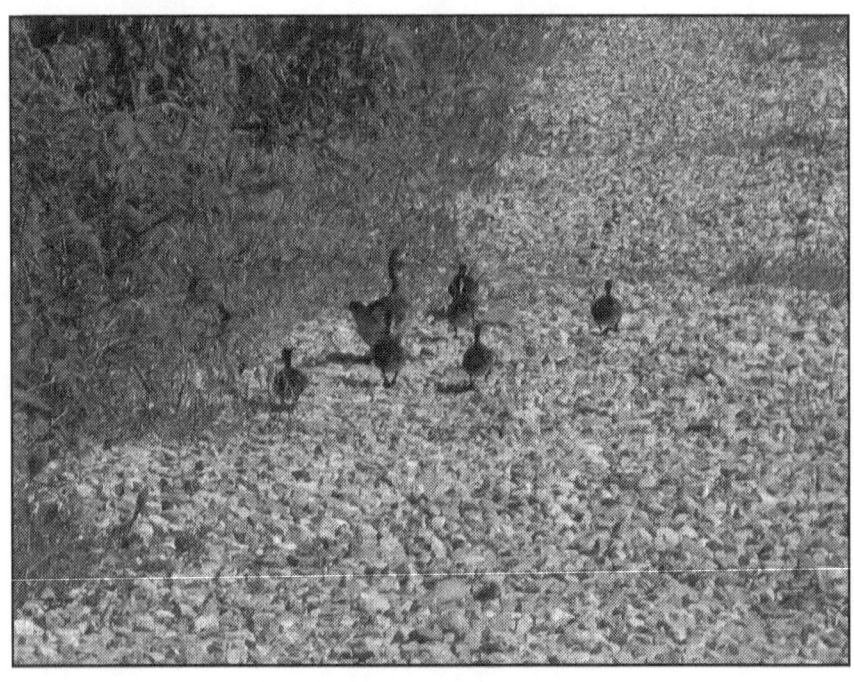

Little Sacrifices
Scene from Tarlton Road, Pickaway County, Ohio -
taken by Amy J. Cooper.

Little Sacrifices

As mothers can,
    And mothers should,
        She carefully guided,
            Her little brood.
Across the road,
    They made their way,
        Carefully following,
            Not knowing today,
A sacrifice sudden,
    Of one of the feather,
        Was the risk unspoken,
            For traveling together.
I came upon them,
    After moments had passed.
        Mamma's eyes met mine,
            The memory forever would last.
A duckling laid still,
    On the center line,
        Gone forever,
            But for memory all time.
We stood silent,
    As the flock gathered 'round.
        So sad in the moment,
            Not one made a sound.
I fell to my knees,
    My heart broken in two,
        Soft prayer was then spoken,
            And then we both knew,
No sacrifice is small,
    All too painfully given,
        And live on in the memories,
            Of those who are left living.

Poetry for the Bradley Cancer Center

Introduction

A historical event took place in Circleville, Ohio in early 2006. The Bradley Cancer Center at Berger Hospital celebrated its official opening. Generosity was shown by many to make this dream come to fruition, and especially so from the Bradley family. This family has been touched many times by the fate of cancer. It is their dream, through their extremely generous and selfless donation, that having a cancer center in Pickaway County, Ohio will enable those who need cancer care be able to get it in their own community.

Before the Bradley Cancer Center opened, much work went into the design in order to make it as comfortable and nurturing a setting as possible. Dr. Jain and his staff were already in place. The challenge was to create a setting that would match their compassion. And that is where I had the privilege of playing a part. I was invited by Wendy Elliott, Executive Director of Pickaway Health Services, to write poetry to match the art chosen for the Bradley Cancer Center in Circleville. She and Connie Kelly also invited me to write for Dr. Jain's office in Grove City.

Most of the art was the work of artists such as Picasso, Norman Rockwell and Monet. I did not seek to gain permission to show their work in The Hills of Circleville. However, some art was that of artists who I have come to know through my work with the ArtsaRound Gallery at Berger. These artists, Mary T. Allen, Elizabeth Campbell and Gayle Cummins, have given me permission to show their work and I am honored to share these pieces with you.

Please enjoy the following pages of poetry and know that, while each piece was written for a specific piece of art, my sister, Wendy Walter, was the true inspiration for my words. A cancer survivor, Wendy is also a fierce champion who would fight the world for her family and is truly an advocate for all of God's creatures. Wendy....these are for you and for all like you who battle cancer – may they all share your courage and attitude.

The Bradley Cancer Center

It is a place of the past,
Of memories growing strong as the trees,
That line the fields, with lovely green leaves,
To honor those who have gone before,
Courageous fighters of legend and lore.

It is a place of the present,
Of fields of hope with flowers that dance,
In the light breeze, their gift is the chance,
The hope that we find when others give,
Their care, their love so we may live.

It is a place of the future,
Of dreams clear as the sky is blue,
That one day, not needed for me or for you,
This place can take another form just as pure,
For the dream is love and the dream is cure.

Just a Man

I am a husband, a father, a brother.
I am the son of one and a friend of another.
I am an athlete, a hunter, a student, a scholar.
        I am many things,
                I am like no other.

I am all of these, but I am just a man.
While fighting this fight, I will do all I can,
To meet each day, to be strong, to be kind,
I will fight this fight, and know this time,
        This battle,
                is yours, is ours, is mine.

I am a husband, a father, a brother.
I am the son of one and the friend of another.
I am a soldier at war, my enemy at the gate.
And I will survive, for this is my fate,
To live my days as
        A husband, a father, a brother.
                The son of one and the friend of another.

Just a Woman

I am a mother, a wife, a daughter.
I am the sister of one, the friend of another.
I am a writer, a cook, I am a gardener.
I dream and I do and give love to others.

I am just a woman, but I am all of these,
I must sail this ship through these troubling seas.
And sail I will, and be all I can be,
That is what you know, that is what is me.

I am a mother, a wife, a daughter.
I am the sister of one, the friend of another.
I will survive this storm and when it is ended,
I will write, cook and see that my garden is tended.

Friends

I really thought that I was fine,
And never planned to look behind.
I found a sunny place to be,
To contemplate the world of me.

When all at once, a friend called out,
A friend I never knew before.
He held out his hand and gave a shout.
First there was one, then there were more.

How interesting, I sat and thought,
What gifts this day to me has brought.
I hadn't realized how great my need,
For caring thoughts and friend's good deed.

But alas it is that now I see,
When contemplating the world of me,
That all these folks, these friends of mine,
Will ease the challenge of this difficult time.

Circle of Friends

I have quite a circle of friends.
Some I've known for many a year,
Some only since that first tear,
When I knew I would need my circle of friends.

I have my circle of friends.
To guide me through the day,
Some live near, and some far away.

I have my circle of friends,
Through it all, we'll hold hands.
We'll laugh and cry,
And try to understand why,

And how, and then,
My circle of friends,
will warm my heart again.
I love my circle of friends.

I Am Strong

I am bright, I am bold,
I am strong, I will be heard.
I'll tell my story, it must be told,
Of how I survived cancer,
And how I grew old.

It thought that it had me,
The battle was won.
But I had just started,
I had just begun.

I underwent treatment,
And made myself strong,
Through modern technology,
And old-fashioned song.
The songs were my prayers,
Sent to Heaven above,
And the song was sung back to me,
It was a message of love.

Yes, I won that battle,
And when it was through,
I was forced into war again,
For a cancer anew.
It came back to find me,
To try to take everything,
But I'm strong like the lily,
And I'll be here every spring.

One Moment

One day at a time,
       Well, that just will not do,
For I shall take mine,
       By a moment or two.

For the first moment today,
       I will watch the morning sun,
Softly sift through my window,
       And not until I am done,
Will I take the next moment,
       To watch my window sill,
              As each plant I have nurtured,
                     Receives its fill,
Of sun, of warmth of a moment in time.
       Alone in this moment, the world is mine.
Yes, a moment or two is what I will take,
       Before I move on,
              My next task for to take.
Now, before I am too much at rest,
       I will tackle the wallpaper.
              I think that is best.
       For what better way,
                     To busy my being, my body and day?
Yes, please take your day one at a time,
       For that is your strength,
              But that is not mine.
I find mine in moments,
       Much like these,
              To cherish and hold,
       And do as I please.

Pieces of Spring

I have pieces of spring.
      Their held in this jar,
            Which had sat plain and empty,
                  When I saw them afar.

Where they beckoned me,
      And they called me by name.
            And since I have picked them,
                  I've not been the same.

My garden's inside now, these tulips divine,
      Stand strong and stand sturdy,
            Their beauty now mine.

The colors of spring, of leaves and new life,
      Red, pink , gold and yellow, and even some white,
            The colors of courage and warmth and sunlight.

Dancing Shoes

Please don't lose another minute lost in those blues,
For far better 'twould be to put on your dancing shoes.
Let us not lose a minute, a moment in time,
Let us glide across the dance floor,
Your hand in mine.

In your arms, I'll look into those eyes I adore,
As we ever so sweetly glide across the floor.
The music so grand as it floats through the air,
Will enchants us with freedom,
We'll dance without care.

Life is to celebrate, to honor, to dance.
Let us not lose this moment, let us not take that chance.
Put on your dancing shoes, don't waste any time.
We'll dance a memory, your heart in mine.

God's Hands

I dream of God's hands,
    Gently tousling my hair,
        And caressing my face,
            As the wind rushes,
                Through my car window.

Free of spirit,
    I travel the winding country roads,
        I have come to know and love.

And so I dream.

Slowly, I awake.
    I am in my favorite, quiet room.
        A window is open,
            And I can hear the birds,
                The soft summer sounds.

At peace, I realize that,
    It matters not,
        That I am without hair,
            For God's hands to tousle.
    A slight breeze comes near,
        And I feel His hands,
            He caresses my face,
                And gives me dreams,
                    Of hair-tousled days to come.

Poppies

Have you ever seen a field of poppies,
Dancing in warm summer breeze?
Tossing their heads as if laughing,
And singing to the nearby trees?

Their vibrant red dancing display,
Pulls at your heart as if to say,
Come join us in this field so bright.
We'll dance and sing into the night.

So that no matter how long, you will not forget,
The feeling of hope that the display had meant,
They invite you to gather them, to take what you need.
There are plenty to share, so no worries of greed.
Put a vase on you table, and fill it with red,
Of lovely wild poppies to dance in your head.

Dream

Whenever the day is too much for me,
Worrying what the future will be.
I close my eyes and dream a dream,
Of bright flower petals and soft lit things.

I seem to float with hardly a care,
With flowers of red, gently fly in the air.
It matters not what this dream may mean.
It brings me peace and tranquility.

And whence from the dream I find I'm awake,
I have greater courage for the next step to take.
For this journey is difficult, and at times it is wondrous,
With light of hope ahead on the road before us.

Autumn

Is this the autumn of my life?
I wonder aloud as to the distance I gaze,
At the festival of colors that fills the autumn days.
Leaves brightly dressed rustle about in the trees,
And the answer is here dancing in the breeze.
It is in the cool wooded scent that fills the air,
It's in the lake and the stream…it is sung everywhere.
This is a time to take comfort, it is the colorful season,
To celebrate life and to know that the reason,
For autumn's colorful delightful display,
Is to prepare us for winter when cold is the day,
When the snow in blankets covers the ground,
Preparing for spring when new strength will abound.
Yes, the crisp autumn wind carries the answer in song,
That the magic around us is what makes us strong,
And prepares us for the future, for life made anew.
This is the journey of healing for me and for you.

Why Me?

You ask me why.
Why me? You say.
How can I answer?
What shall I say?

Because you chose to see things your way.
You chose to fight, to seize the day.
When others laid down to rest,
You were strong and stood the test,
Of challenge, of time,
of pain, of mind.

When others saw fields filled with weeds,
You saw poppies galore dancing in the breeze.
When others laid down to rest in bed,
You gathered flowers of yellow and red.

Why me? You ask.
Why me? You say.
Why have you survived,
When others have not?
The answer my friend, is within your mind.
You saw the victory before its time.
You chose to live, you valiantly fought.
You saw the poppies,
Where others saw naught.

Lake of Irises

You see a garden with irises of blue.
I see a lake with a boat made for two.
You see the flowers sway to and fro.
I see the tide as it waves high to low.

You see a garden, locked on the land.
I see a lake and fishing so grand.
You pluck a flower to take with you.
I cast a line for a fish or for two.

No matter what we see, you and I,
We'll be doing so 'neath the same blue sky.
And when the day must come to end,
We'll still have each other to call friend.

A Field of Summer

A field of summer,
A memory held dear,
For when I am lonely,
And need to feel you near.

A sea of flowers,
Dancing in the breeze,
A warm summer day,
When all was at ease.

This is my memory,
Of a day spent with you,
That keeps me warm and smiling,
When I begin to feel blue.

They Can't Take This From Me

They can't take this from me,
Try as they might,
This glorious morning,
This beautiful sight.

The sun how it rises,
Off to the east,
As I cast out my line,
In search of a feast.

For there's nothing more filling,
Then food by your hand,
Through hunting, farming or fishing,
On God's lakes, ponds and land.

They can't take away,
A memory so divine,
As fishing at sunrise,
And casting your line.

The sounds, scents, the sights and the taste,
Are mine for eternity, no moment I'll waste.
I'll live this great life and build memories each day.
They can't take these from me, for forever they'll stay.

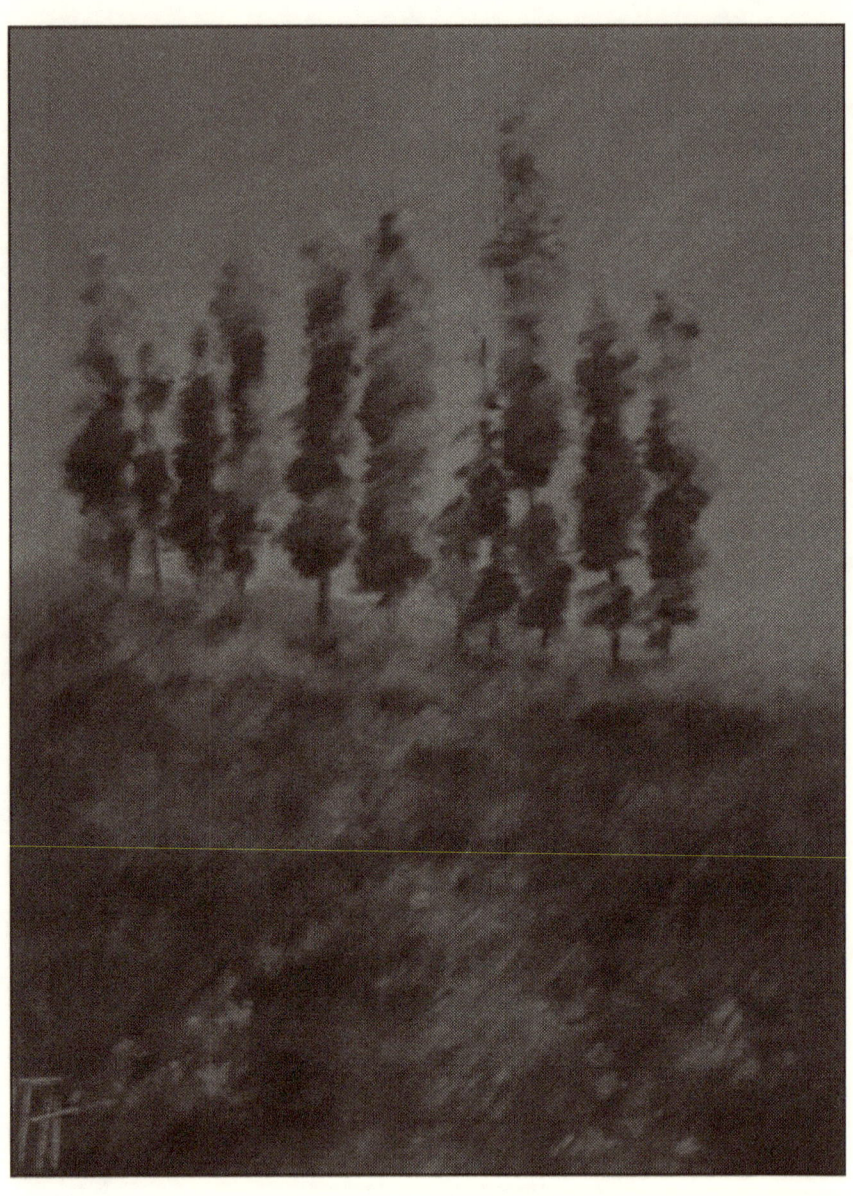

View of Spring Poplars (for poem titled "If I Could Paint a Picture")

Artist: Mary T. Allen from Dublin, Ohio

If I Could Paint a Picture

If I could paint a picture,
I know what I would do.
I'd paint a soft, spring daybreak,
Fields fresh with morning dew.

Pastel would be the colors,
To elegantly display,
My belief in the future,
And my hope for today.

If I could paint a picture,
I know what it would be,
A warm field of hope and love,
With strong, proud poplar tree.

The poplars so straight and tall,
Reaching up to the sky of blue,
Would touch the hands of God, and then,
Fill me with hope renewed.

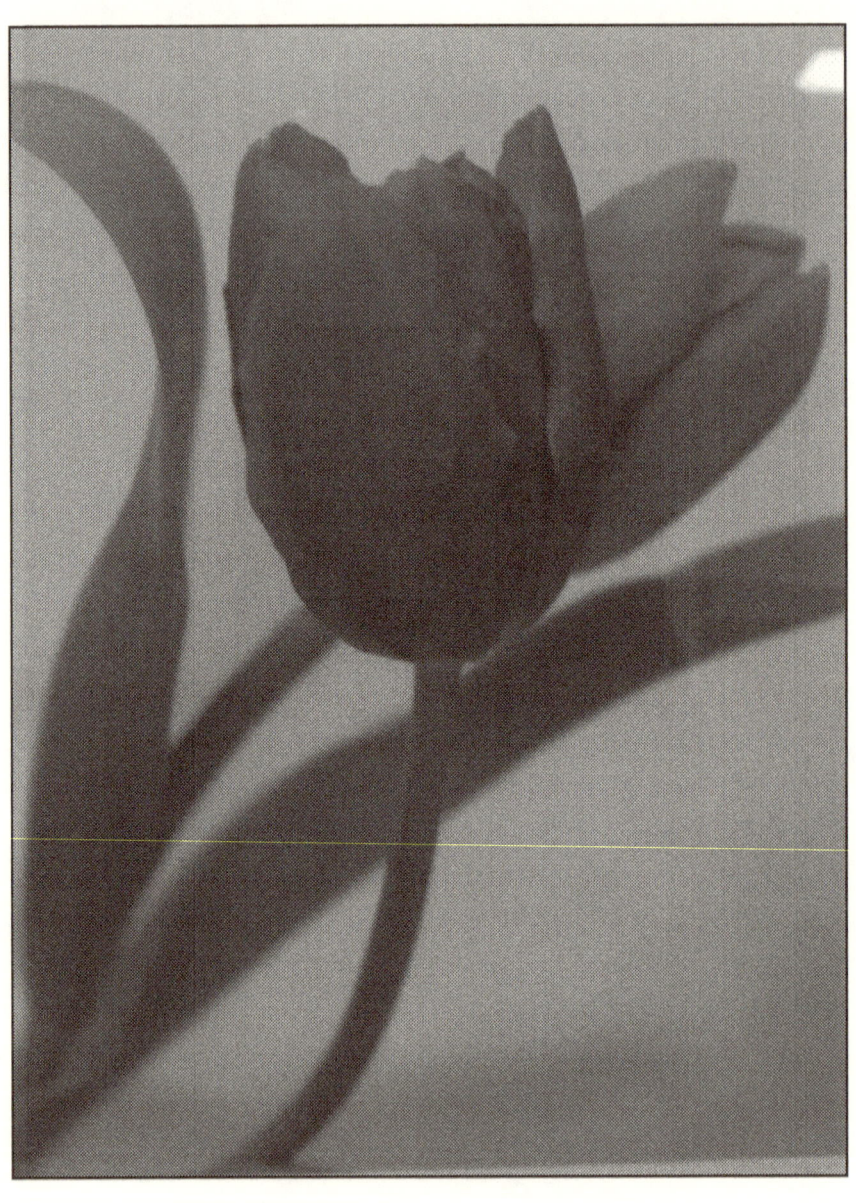

Two Tulips (for poem titled "Two Lives")
Artist: Elizabeth Campbell from Glen Falls, New York
(www.elizabethcampbellphotography.com)

Two Lives

Two lives entwined,
Your heart in mine.

We stand as one,
The battle begun.

Side by side,
We'll seize each day.
Through prayer and love,
We'll know the way.

'Though delicate,
With petals soft and fair,
Our spirit and strength,
Is beyond compare.

Our petals may softly fall upon the dirt,
But our roots hold tight to Mother Earth.

For petals are but for the show,
And true beauty lives within.
And love and spirit still will grow,
When petals are blown in the wind.

For the pleasure of the colors,
Our petals in delight display,
Will once again be with us,
One warm and sunny day.

And then we'll stand in the spring sunshine,
Your love and mine, our hearts entwined.
With petals seemingly frail, and yet so strong,
The battle but a memory, the battle we have won.

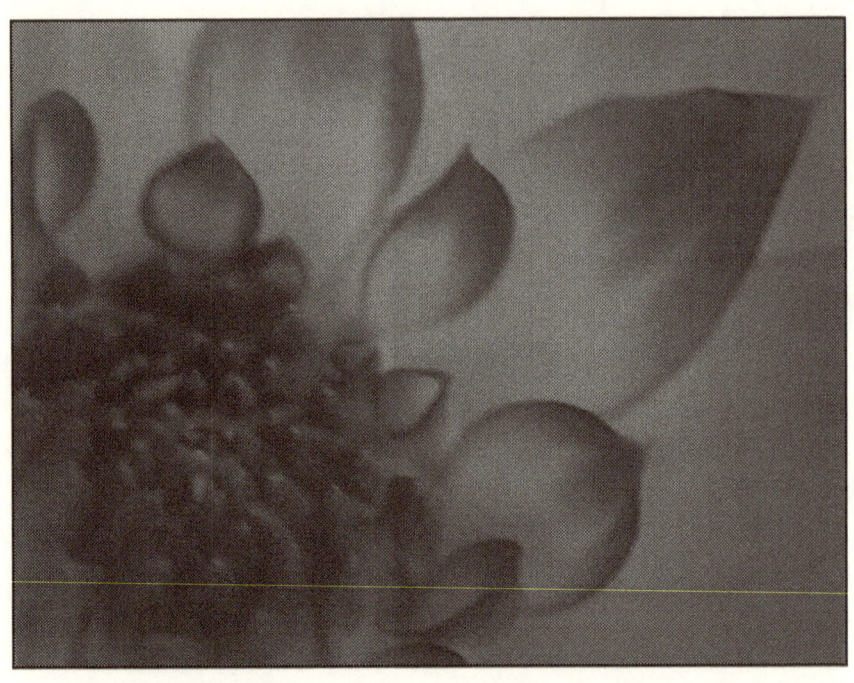

Glowing Dahlia (for poem titled "You are Everywhere")
Artist: Elizabeth Campbell from Glen Falls, New York
(www.elizabethcampbellphotography.com)

You are Everywhere

There you are. I see you there,
Standing there, as still as the air.
You are everywhere, you are all around,
In the soft-lit petals of the dahlia strong,
In the melody of mourning dove,
That fills me with peace and strength and love.
You are in the glow of the moon at night,
And in the dawn, at the first of light.
You are in the smell of fresh cut grass,
You are here for me, my strength will last.
Today, 'tis true that I must fight.
But, not alone; with you by my side.
I'll glow like the dahlia, face to the sun,
Breathing in the warmth 'til day is done,
Breathing in your love 'til this battle is won.

The Peaceful Path

Down through the meadow and beyond the trees,
    Winds the path that is peaceful,
        Which sets my mind to ease.

Amongst the poppies and Queen Anne's lace,
    Through the twists and the turns,
        My mind wanders beyond this place.

I can feel the warmth of the setting sun,
    As its golden kisses,
        Tell me the day is done.

Another day promised, another day lived,
    Another day knowing I have more love to give.
Though tired and quite weary, I am never alone,
    For the path that is peaceful will bring my heart home.

Never Alone

It seems in moments like these,
     When stormy clouds toss the seas,
That cold and grey my thoughts should be,
     As I would wallow in my misery.

Yet as I feel the mist of rain,
     My thoughts drift far from my pain,
For the rain and clouds are God's work as well.
     For the wind in the clouds sings the waves to swell,
And the rain kisses the buds so the flowers will grow.

     And I find I'm at peace for this I know,
That no matter where my mind may roam,
     I am always loved. I am never alone.

My Mind's Lake

Whenever it becomes too much for me,
  I've had all that I can take.
I close my eyes and deeply breathe,
  And my mind goes to the lake.

The soft hissing sound,
  of water kissing shore,
Fills me with such calmness,
  I know that I will endure.

The golden grass softly sways.
  The sun gently caresses my face.
I pray this peace within me stays,
  My mind's lake, my serenity place.

Meadow Song

The flowers are lovely with colors of bright,
        Why am I saddened by this beautiful sight?
Perhaps I'm consumed in this moment of thought,
        Of all of my dreams; were they all for naught?

I feel the tug of the flowers as they sing to me,
        Yet I struggle to stay in my own pity.
True, I deserve to be sad and fearful at best,
        But the flowers are calling; they won't give it a rest.

"All right," I say quietly for no one to hear,
        I'll take this moment and let go of my fear.
I'll feel the slight breeze as it touches my face,
        And know God's love is here, it is every place.

I'll breathe in the moment, and hear the birds sing,
        I'll let the love fill my soul as it makes my heart ring.
For no matter what will come in time,
        The sunshine, the flowers and God's love are mine.

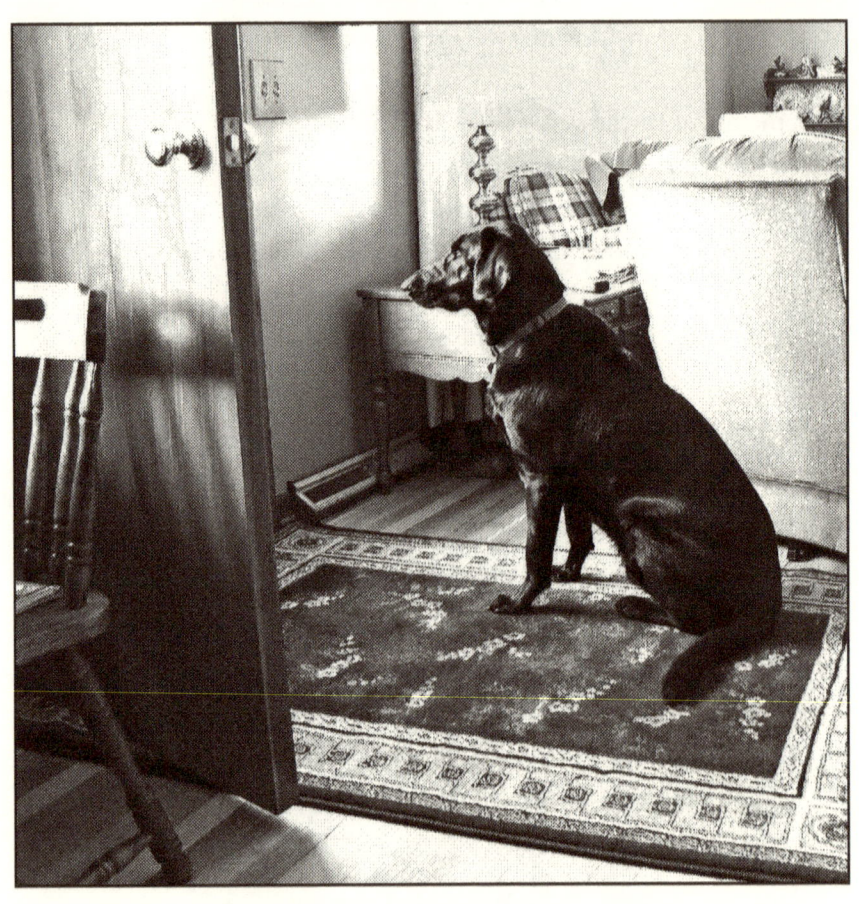

Waiting (for poem titled the same)
Artist: Gayle Cummins from Ashville, Ohio
(www.gaylecphotography.com)

Waiting

It really doesn't matter,
     Wherever you may go,
I will always be here waiting,
     Right by the open door.

You may have had a bad day,
     You may be tired and worn,
But no matter what you do or say,
     To you my heart is sworn.

It matters not how you may look,
     Or if you take to bed,
For patience is mine, I wrote the book,
     And I'm best at cuddling, I've heard it said.

So worry not your weary mind,
     I'm right here waiting, I have the time.
For me these things come ever so naturally,
     Forever to wait and love you unconditionally.

Mashed Potatoes

These are the poems which didn't quite fit in any of the other chapters. I know I could call this section miscellaneous, potpourri, or cornucopia. All good words to be sure...but those you would expect. So...here it is - I shall close *The Hills of Circleville* with a small serving of "mashed potatoes."

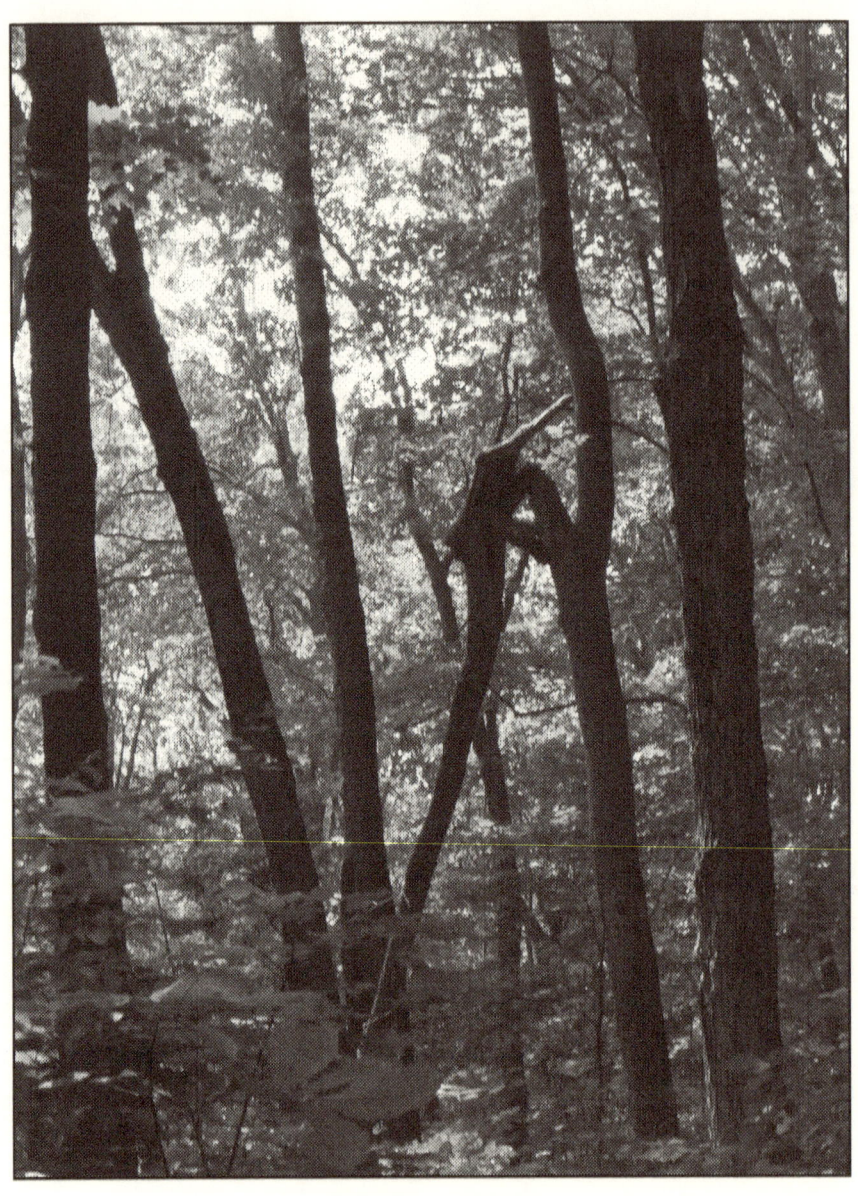

Without a Sound
Scene from Hargus Lake, Pickaway County, Ohio -
taken by Amy J. Cooper.

Without a Sound

If a tree falls with no one around,
      Is it loud like the thunder,
Or does it utter no sound?

And I wonder when I fall to my knees,
      Will my heart scream in silence,
Amidst the old pine trees?

Will I leave this place in the quiet of night?
      Will I be noticed when I'm no longer nearby?
Or will I quietly lie, like the tree on the ground,
      With no one remembering I was ever around?

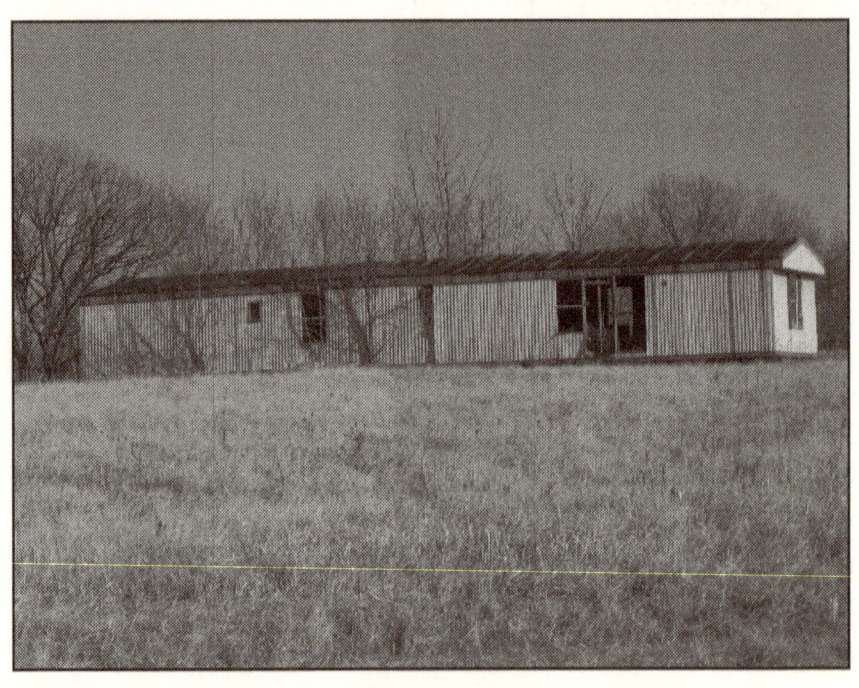

Abandoned
Scene from Dozier Road - taken by Amy J. Cooper.

Abandoned

Who left you here amidst the weeds,
      Abandoned and hidden among the trees?
Did you serve your purpose 'til the last day,
      They tossed you aside and threw you away?

You were home to them, you were family,
      How could they leave you, didn't they see,
That homes, unlike people, are always around,
      They love you and hold you and keep you warm?

Ah, but alas you've been tossed aside,
      Down in the meadow in the tall grass you hide.
And I will never forget the feeling I hold,
      As I gaze down at you and you fill my soul,
With stories of love,
         And memories not mine,
            Not mine, yet I'll keep and hold them near,
               For 'til now I've had no such memories,
                  To love and hold so dear.

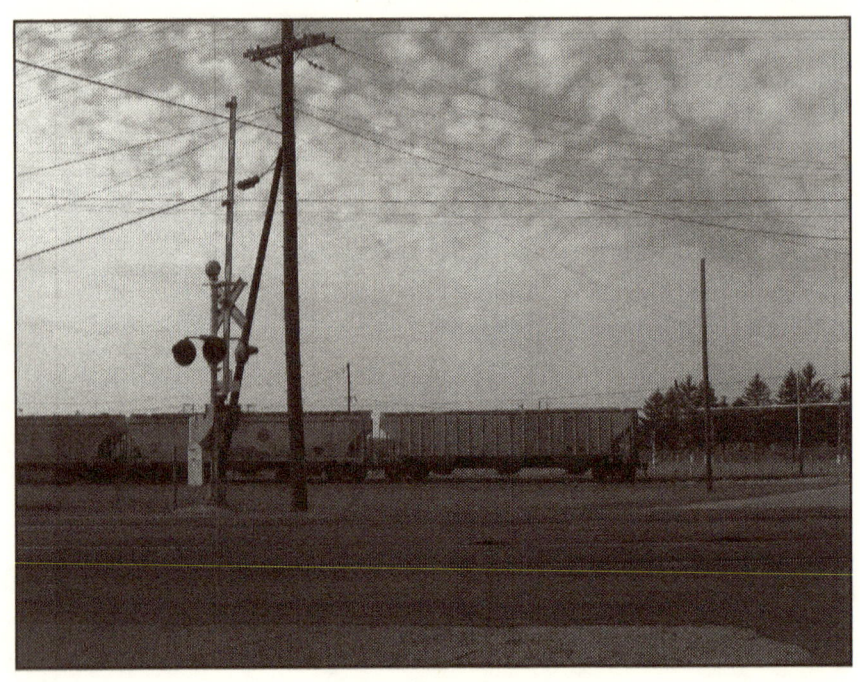

Evening Train
Scene from Circleville, Ohio - taken by Amy J. Cooper.

Evening Train

Deep in the summer night,
 When the moon is new,
I can hear the whistle blowin'
 As a lonely light comes into view.

How hauntingly familiar,
 The melody refrain,
The rhythm of the night song,
 The romance of the train.

And as my heart takes flight,
 To places far away,
The train passes in the night,
 Another dream before the dawn of day.

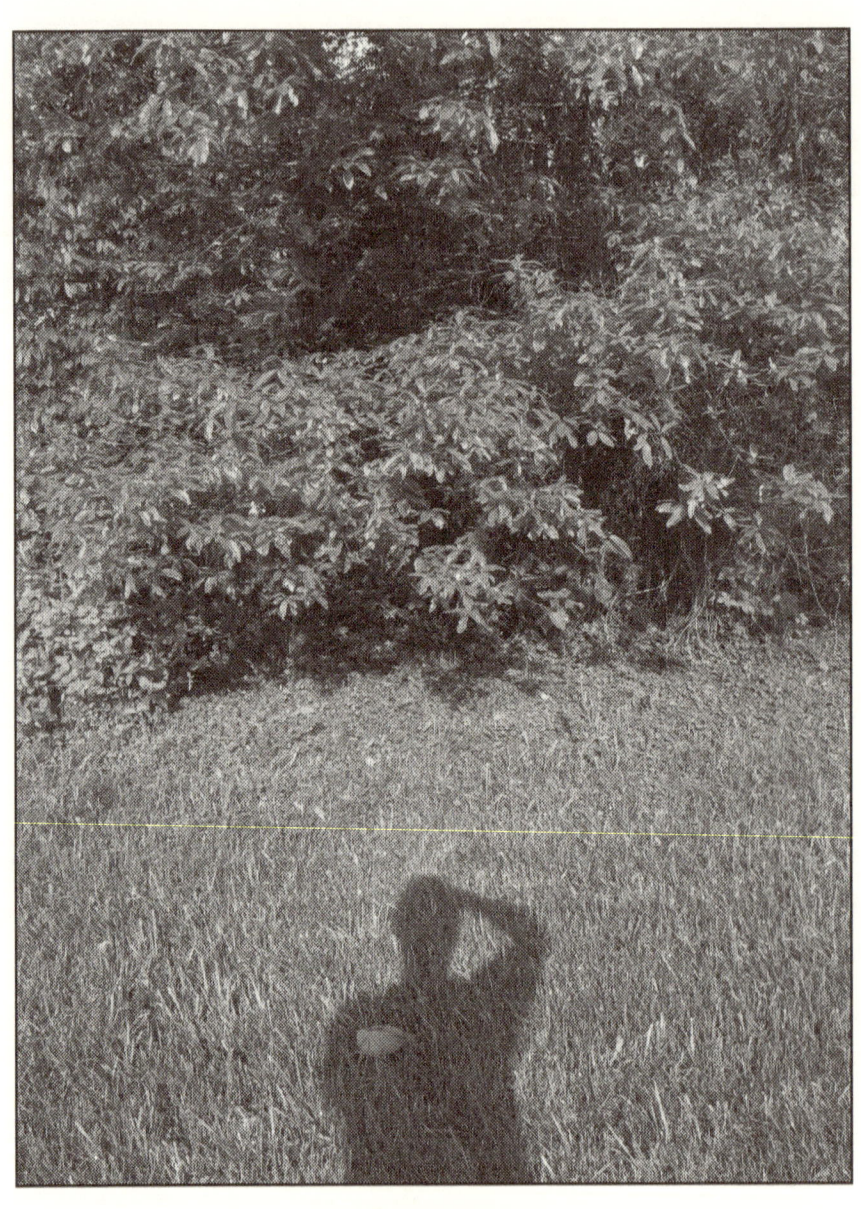

My Shadow
Scene from author's home - taken by Amy J. Cooper.

My Shadow

It follows me wherever I roam,
    Uninvited, it still comes nigh.
        No matter how far I am from home,
            I feel it near and I hear its sigh.

Sometimes when weary have grown my thoughts,
    And I feel all I've done, I've done for naught,
        I turn my back to the setting sun,
            Another day with no battle won.

And just as I think with disbelief,
    That this world is filled with too much grief,
        My shadow, that hidden part of me,
            Stands to the front and takes the lead.

Then into the night I know I must follow,
    'Til shadow fades into dreams of morrow.

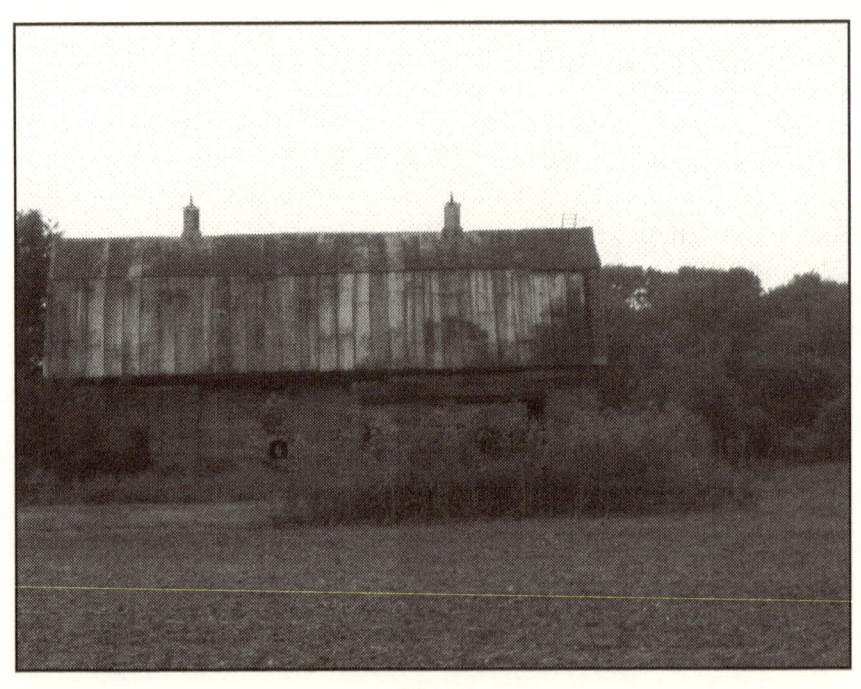

The Child Within
Scene from Old Tarlton Pike - taken by Amy J. Cooper.

The Child Within

Just like me, it stands still and strong,
Weathered wood, wrinkled skin,
For a life lived long.

The tin roof holds tight,
The rust serves as token,
Of heart still whole,
Though so many times broken.

Tired and worn,
Though we may appear,
There is no call, nor need,
For shedding a tear.

For though we are tattered,
We're weathered and worn,
Inside is the child,
Who never has grown.

And if you look closely,
Through the door to my mind,
You'll see my rhythm.
You'll learn of my rhyme.

The child within us,
Like roped tire for swing,
Is what makes joy of living,
And lets spirits take wing.

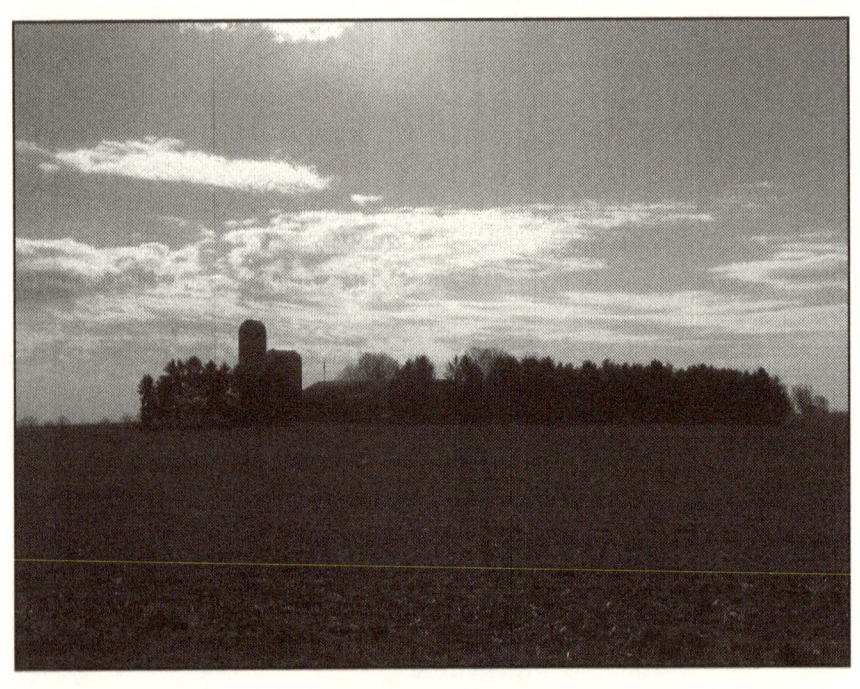

Finding the Peace
Scene from Old Tarlton Pike - taken by Amy J. Cooper.

Finding the Peace

Standing still and silent, across the open field,
    If able to speak to me,
        What would your stories yield?

Did you see the trauma of World War II?
    If so, then you have stood,
        The Korean War too.

Have you ever seen a time of peace?
        Ever a time when war,
            Had come to cease?

I wonder as I see you there,
    Was there a time with peace in the air?
        A time when children without care,
        Played in your fields, laughter everywhere?

Perhaps all along I have been wrong,
    I think as I watch you standing strong.
For in God's world, all things remain,
    The laughter, the tears, the sun and the rain.
His Blessing is strong and seen from afar,
    It is finding the peace during the war.

During the summer of 2005, I was among a group of published writers who were invited to attend a Writer's Ink event at the beautiful Thurber House in Columbus, Ohio. Strangers became friends as together we baked in what was an enchanting, yet very hot room. A bond formed in those kinds of circumstances is a strong bond. These friends, the Sauna Friends as we now call ourselves, are traveling to events to promote writing, not only through our published works, but also to engage audiences in discussions about the art of writing and the joy of reading.

Sauna Friends

Turning the pages,
RM caught me by surprise.
Death of an Agent,
Right before mine eyes.

Turning for something sweeter,
Some call to rejoice,
And there with Nancy's words,
I feel and I *Hear His Voice.*

With Jerry's thoughts on life's choices,
I'm *Jumping with Joy* at the pleasure,
Of finding the truth,
All things of love our life to measure.

Sandra's voice is a melody,
A *Song of Turand.*
Robert brings *Sunshine for the Soul,*
Words of poetry surpassing grand.

In *Light Years,* Robin spins a tale so fine,
Debbie's *Forever Kind of Love,*
Is ours, the Sauna Friends, for all time.

Epilogue

Epilogue – what an interesting word, and so appropriate for the last words of *The Hills of Circleville*. It fits for the traditional use of the word, for these are my closing comments. No more photographs to take. No more poetry to spill from my pen. This is it. A time to stop writing and let it be, only to hope I have somehow conveyed the love I feel for the place I now call my home. To be so inspired that something so ordinary as my shadow, or a tree branch on my land could bring words of rhythm and rhyme to my mind is living a dream.

Epilogue in its traditional use is not what comes first to my mind though. For it is the prefix of the word, "epi" on which I focus as I am writing this last page. Epi – surface – yes, that is really all I've done. For every moment I thought I was finished with *The Hills of Circleville*, I would take yet another photograph, which would inspire yet another poem. "Now, I'm done." Another poem later, I would whisper, "yes, now I am done." Two poems later, another picture…and so it went on. Today, I surrender to the prefix "epi." For all these pages later, I have only scratched the surface.

In closing, yet on the surface, I leave you with these words:

Live every day as though your last,
    when others hurt you,
        leave behind the past.

Let the little things be your every day thrills,
    and let your heart soar
        when you gaze at the hills.

www.ingramcontent.com/pod-product-compliance
Lightning Source LLC
Chambersburg PA
CBHW032019170526
45157CB00002B/774